# Challenge

## Level 5

## Teacher's Annotated Edition

A Division of The McGraw-Hill Companies

Columbus, Ohio

**www.sra4kids.com**

*SRA/McGraw-Hill*

*A Division of The McGraw-Hill Companies*

Copyright © 2002 by SRA/McGraw-Hill.

Send all inquiries to:
SRA/McGraw-Hill
8787 Orion Place
Columbus, OH 43240-4027

Printed in the United States of America.

ISBN  0-07-572055-8

  2 3 4 5 6 7 8 9 QPD 07 06 05 04 03 02

# Table of Contents

## Unit 5 — Going West

## Unit 6 — Journeys and Quests

**COMPREHENSION**

# ▶ Drawing Conclusions

**Drawing Conclusions** means using information in a text or a story to make a statement about a person, event, or thing. Read each passage below and, in the margins of this page, *draw* what the text tells you to. Then, draw a conclusion or make a statement about what you have drawn.

1. Max bought his mother a timely gift for the kitchen. (Draw a circle with a plus sign in the middle, making sure its ends touch the edges of the circle. Make a big dot in the middle where the lines cross. Write the number twelve at the top of the circle and a six at the bottom.)

   What conclusion can you draw about what the gift is? What information in the text supports your answer?

   The gift is a clock. The object has the numbers twelve and

   six on it and the text says that it is timely and goes in the

   kitchen.

2. Pam and Will's Uncle Bill lives in a cool place. (Draw two horizontal wavy lines, one right above the other. Just above the two wavy lines, draw a horizontal rectangle. Then, just above the rectangle, almost touching it, draw a tall triangle.)

   What conclusion can you draw about where the place is? What information in the text supports your answer?

   The place is a boat or on the water. The object looks like

   a boat on water and the text says it is a cool place. Water

   is generally cool.

   On a separate sheet of paper, write a new passage (a clue and drawing instructions) for an object from "Class President." Give it to a classmate and let him or her draw a conclusion.

   Answers will vary.

# ▶ The /a/ Sound

**SPELLING**

## Pronunciation Strategy
Write the words from the list that have the /a/ sound.

| accident | addition | airplane | calculate | gable |
|----------|----------|----------|-----------|-------|
| galaxy | knapsack | label | radio | rapid |

1. accident
2. addition
3. calculate
4. galaxy
5. knapsack
6. rapid

## Rhyming Strategy
Write words with the /a/ sound that rhyme with the words below.

Answers will vary.

7. brass   _____
8. dance   _____
9. grand   _____
10. plaid   _____
11. thank   _____
12. strap   _____

# ▶ Discovering Word Meanings

**Tell what each of the underlined words means based on what you know about the word or the words surrounding it.**

**1.** I cut my finger on the rock's <u>jagged</u> edge.

**having sharp or uneven edges**

**2.** I used the <u>mallet</u> to hit the ball when we played croquet.

**hammer used in games**

**3.** Peter tried to <u>salvage</u> the game by hitting a home run, but we still lost.

**save from loss**

**4.** Kwan <u>valiantly</u> tried to save the drowning child.

**bravely, courageously**

**5.** I could not <u>fathom</u> why anyone would not want to play basketball.

**understand**

**6.** When he saw the snake, he was <u>paralyzed</u> with fear and could not move another inch.

**unable to move**

**7.** Before the meeting began, the people <u>assembled</u> in the room.

**gathered**

**8.** I got a new coat because my old one looked too <u>shabby</u>.

**worn, faded, or dingy**

VOCABULARY

Name _____ Date _____

# ▶ Nouns

▶ **Fill in the blanks with nouns.**   **Answers will vary.**

_____ was a good day for _____. She got up early

and cleaned her _____. Then she went to the _____

to play. At lunch, she had _____ and _____ to eat.

After lunch, she read a book about _____. Since the day

was hot, _____ went for a swim in the _____. To

end the day, _____ asked _____ to watch a video

with her family. Her day had been so full that as soon as

_____ went to _____ she fell asleep. That night, she

dreamed of going to the _____.

▶ **Choose the correct plurals. Use the dictionary if necessary.**

1. One crisis, several (crisises, (crises))

2. One son-in-law, three ((sons-in-law) son-in-laws)

3. One sheep, many ((sheep) sheeps)

4. One alumnus, four (alumnae, (alumni))

5. One radio, both (radioes, (radios))

6. One country, a few ((countries) countrys)

7. One bunch, two ((bunches) bunchs)

8. One quiz, five (quizes, (quizzes))

9. One crash, ten ((crashes) crashs)

**GRAMMAR AND USAGE**

**UNIT 1**  Cooperation and Competition • **Lesson 2** *The Marble Champ*

## ▶ Making Inferences

Based on descriptions of two characters' interactions with each other, readers can often make inferences about their relationship. In "The Marble Champ," Lupe's father gives up his plans to play racquetball with a friend in order to go with Lupe to the marbles championship. From this, one can infer that Lupe's father takes an interest in what she does. Review the story further and use both information in the text and your personal knowledge about parent-child relationships to make three inferences about the relationship between Lupe and her father. Explain what information led you to make each inference.

**Answers may vary. Possible answers are shown.**

**Inference 1:** Lupe and her father have a close relationship.

**Explanation:** Lupe's father builds her a shelf for awards. They go places and do things together, such as roller skating.

**Inference 2:** Lupe's father gives her emotional and practical support.

**Explanation:** He rigs the lights in the backyard so Lupe can practice after dark for the marbles championship and encourages her when she has a tough opponent.

**Inference 3:** Lupe's father is proud of her.

**Explanation:** He smiles and hugs Lupe when she wins, and he feels she should display her trophy in the restaurant after she wins the championship.

COMPREHENSION

# ▶The /e/ Sound

**Visualization Strategy**
**Fill in the blank with the correct spelling for the /e/ sound.**

1. I don't know wh_e_ther to have the spaghetti or ravioli.

2. The w_ea_ther report said it would be rainy and dreary.

3. The sun gives off _e_nergy in the form of heat.

4. The horse's saddle is made of l_ea_ther.

5. We ran for sh_e_lter when it began to rain.

**Visualization Strategy**
**Use the code to write the letters of the clue.**
**Then fill in the rest of the word with the correct**
**spelling of the /e/ sound.**

| 1 | 2 | 3 | 4 | 5 | 6 | 7 | 8 | 9 | 10 | 11 | 12 | 13 | 14 |
|---|---|---|---|---|---|---|---|---|----|----|----|----|----|
| a | c | d | g | i | j | l | n | o | r | s | t | u | y |

6. __c__ __o__ __n__ __n__ __e__ __c__ __t__
    2   9   8   8      2   12

7. __j__ __ea__ __l__ __o__ __u__ __s__
    6      7   9  13  11

8. __c__ __a__ __l__ __e__ __n__ __d__ __a__ __r__
    2   1   7      8   3   1  10

9. __d__ __i__ __g__ __e__ __s__ __t__
    3   5   4      11  12

10. __s__ __t__ __ea__ __d__ __y__
     11  12      3   14

**SPELLING**

**UNIT 1** Cooperation and Competition • **Lesson 2** *The Marble Champ*

# ▶Context Clues

**VOCABULARY**

▶ **Write the letter of the correct meaning of the underlined words. Use context clues to help you.**

Scientists can visit the deepest parts of the ocean only in equipment that is made to fit the <u>conditions</u> there. They <u>descend</u> to the sea floor in ocean capsules built specially to explore underwater.

1. __b__ *conditions*
   **a.** sea plants
   **b.** environment
   **c.** wetness
   **d.** sand at the bottom of the ocean

2. __c__ *descend*
   **a.** to go up
   **b.** to swim
   **c.** to go down
   **d.** to make ripples

▶ **Fill in the word that best fits each sentence using the words and definitions below.**

| | |
|---|---|
| **tremendous:** | of great size |
| **restless:** | not still |
| **appoint:** | to name for an office or position |
| **methods:** | ways of doing things |
| **discussion:** | the act of talking about ideas |

3. The ____restless____ sea kept me awake all night.

4. Congress delayed the vote because more ____discussion____ was needed.

5. Hurricanes create ____tremendous____ waves.

6. The President ____appoints____ his advisers.

7. The President's advisers help him decide the best ____methods____ for leading the country.

Name ______________________________ Date ____________



# Pronouns

**Choose the correct pronoun.**

1. It was (I, me) who bought the candy.
2. (He, Him) and (I, me) are friends.
3. (She, Her) and (I, me) belong to the same organization.
4. Please let (we, us) go with you.
5. Bob invited (they, them) to a party.
6. (Its, It's) leg was broken in three places.
7. We are going to (your, you're) house after the movie.
8. (Their, They're) helping us rake leaves.
9. (Their, They're) new car is a convertible.
10. (Its, It's) time for (your, you're) nap.

**Correct the pronoun usage in this paragraph.**

Jack and I
One afternoon me and Jack decided to have a
We our
party. Us invited all the boys from their soccer team.
them their
We called they at they're homes. Everyone could come
He Jack and I
except Tom. Him had a dental appointment. I and Jack
We
planned several games. They also went shopping for
we
snacks. When the boys arrived it was raining, but us
had fun anyway.

# Author's Point of View

Imagine that you have been asked by a juggler, a person who juggles objects, to write the copy for a flyer explaining what and how she juggles. First, the juggler wants you to come and watch her perform. After watching, you start writing your copy and find that you can't decide whether to write it from the first-or third-person point of view. You decide to write a draft both ways. Write your drafts below. **Answers will vary.**

**COMPREHENSION**

### Third-Person Point of View

_____

_____

_____

_____

_____

### First-Person Point of View

_____

_____

_____

_____

_____

# ▶The /o/ and /aw/ Sounds

**Visualization Strategy**
**Fill in the blanks with the correct /o/ or /aw/ spelling.**

1. The old man h___o___bbled down the street.

2. When I won the gold medal, I qu___a___lified for the state championship.

3. The bright pink house with the turquoise shutters is g___au___dy.

4. Sean hung his l___au___ndry out to dry.

5. The patriots t___augh___t us to fight for this country.

**Pronunciation Strategy**
**Write the words from the list that have the /o/ or /aw/ sound.**

| | | | | |
|---|---|---|---|---|
| astronaut | boycott | courtesy | cyclone | haughty |
| monstrous | photograph | process | throughout | wrought |

6. astronaut          9. boycott

7. haughty          10. monstrous

8. process          11. wrought

SPELLING

**VOCABULARY**

# ▶ Word Parts

▶ Tell what the word part means by looking at the words and definitions below.

1. **subheading:** a heading under another heading
   **subway:** an underground railway
   **subplot:** a plot less important than the main plot

   What does the prefix *sub*-mean? <u>under or less than</u>

   Write three other words with the prefix *sub*-. <u>Possible answers:</u>
   <u>subscript, submarine, substandard, subtitle, suburb,</u>
   <u>subject.</u>

2. **portable:** able to be carried
   **transport:** to carry across or over
   **important:** to carry a lot of weight

   What does the root *port* mean? <u>to carry, bring</u>

   Write three other words with the root *port*. <u>Possible answers:</u>
   <u>import, export, porter, portfolio.</u>

▶ Write words using the following word parts. The meanings of the parts are given. Tell the meaning of your new words.

| | | |
|---|---|---|
| *con* (together) | *aud* (to hear) | *ible* (form of able) |
| *de* (undo) | *struct* (to build) | |

3. <u>audible</u>        <u>able to hear</u>
4. <u>construct</u>       <u>to build by putting things together</u>
5. <u>destruct</u>        <u>to undo the structure of</u>

**UNIT I** Cooperation and Competition • **Lesson 3** *Juggling*

# ▶Verbs

▶ **Change the past-tense verbs in the paragraph to present-tense verbs.**

     fish
The Eskimos fished for herring, salmon, and other

    use
fish. They used the fish meat to eat. Eskimos also

make                     sell
made the fat into oil for fuel. They sold the fish to

           want                       get
companies that wanted to buy them. The Eskimos got

                                 dry
a high price for some of the fish. Sometimes they dried

              eat
some of the fish and ate it during the winter.

▶ **Change these present tense verbs to past tense.**

1. learn   **learned**         6. live   **lived**

2. dry   **dried**         7. catch   **caught**

3. wake   **woke**         8. do   **did**

4. bring   **brought**         9. help   **helped**

5. teach   **taught**         10. put   **put**

▶ **Change these present tense verbs to future.**

11. run   **will run**

12. jump   **will jump**

13. stop   **will stop**

**GRAMMAR AND USAGE**

# ▶Figurative Language

**WRITER'S CRAFT**

**Use figurative language in the following exercises.**

Answers will vary.

1. In personification, an animal or nonliving thing is compared to a human by giving it human characteristics. Write a paragraph about an animal you feel is most like your personality.

   Possible Answer: *The cat looked at the empty water bowl and complained loudly. The cat was disgusted by the lack of attention to his needs.*

   _____

   _____

   _____

2. The comparison in a metaphor is less direct than in a simile because it does not use the words *like* or *as*. Read this metaphor and answer the questions below.

   *The world is nothing but an endless seesaw.*
   —Michel de Montaigne

   Do you think the world is nothing but a seesaw? If so, in what way? If not, what would you compare the world to?

   Possible Answers: *Yes, the world is nothing but a seesaw because things go up and down or alternate. What is popular one year won't be the next.*

# ▶Sequence

Think of all the words and phrases you know that indicate a time of day, an amount of time, or an order in which events take place. Using those words, write a poem about time. You might describe what it feels like to have to wait for something, write about different ways to use time, or tell how time seems to pass slowly or quickly in different situations. Remember to use time words and order words or phrases in your poem.

Answers will vary.

_____

_____

_____

_____

_____

_____

_____

_____

_____

_____

_____

_____

**COMPREHENSION**

# ▶The /i/ Sound

SPELLING

**Pronunciation Strategy**
Write the word that matches each respelling.

1.  /mith/  <u>myth</u>
2.  /gilt/  <u>guilt</u>
3.  /in' stingkt/  <u>instinct</u>
4.  /mis' chif/  <u>mischief</u>
5.  /jim' nast/  <u>gymnast</u>
6.  /mis' əl/  <u>missile</u>
7.  /ish' o͞o/  <u>issue</u>
8.  /tip' i kəl/  <u>typical</u>
9.  /bī' si kəl/  <u>bicycle</u>
10. /bis' kit/  <u>biscuit</u>

**Pronunciation Strategy**
Fill in the blank with a word that has the /i/ sound.
Answers may vary. Possible answers are shown.

11. It is against the law to <u>litter</u>, but sometimes people throw things out their car window anyway.

12. When I finish writing, I am going to <u>publish</u> my book.

13. My favorite class is <u>physical</u> education.

14. Dinosaurs became <u>extinct</u> a long time ago.

15. The fire <u>extinguisher</u> is on the wall in case of emergency.

16. The word antidisestablishmentarianism has 12 <u>syllables</u>.

# ▶Using the Dictionary

▶Find the following words in your dictionary. Write the number of syllables in the blanks.

1. asylum    <u>3</u>

2. commerce    <u>2</u>

3. phenomenon    <u>4</u>

4. sculpture    <u>2</u>

▶Write the definition of *attend* that tells what a person might do to a sick person.

5. <u>to care for</u>

▶Tell what word you would need to look up to find each of the following words in a dictionary.

6. celebrates <u>celebrate</u>

7. forging <u>forge</u>

8. friendlier <u>friendly</u>

9. greatness <u>great</u>

▶Write a dictionary entry for each of the following words. Do not use your dictionary. The first one is done for you. Sample answers shown. Students may not include all the meanings of the words.

10. contain <u>con·tain (kən tān′) *verb* to have in it</u>

11. simple <u>sim·ple (sim′pəl) *adjective* easy</u>

12. treasure <u>treas·ure (trezh′er) *noun* something that is valued</u>

**VOCABULARY**

**UNIT I** Cooperation and Competition • **Lesson 4** *The Abacus Contest*

# ▶Kinds of Sentences

**GRAMMAR AND USAGE**

**Identify these sentences and add correct end punctuation.**

1. Chinatown has the best restaurants in the city.  **Declarative**

2. Can you name the four food groups?  **Interrogative**

3. Wash your hands with soap and water.  **Imperative**

4. The house is on fire!  **Exclamatory**

5. The surprise party began promptly at noon.  **Declarative**

6. A tornado warning has been issued!/.  **Exclamatory/Declarative**

7. Clean your room, mop the kitchen floor, and rake the leaves.  **Imperative**

8. How many times have you seen that movie?  **Interrogative**

9. Change this declarative sentence to an interrogative sentence.
   **Bob wrote a newspaper editorial about a political candidate.**

   **Did Bob write a newspaper editorial about a political**

   **candidate?**

10. Change this interrogative sentence to an imperative sentence.
    **Will you please close the screen door?**

    **Please close the screen door.**

11. Change this imperative sentence to a declarative sentence.
    **Give me the answer key to the test.**

    **She gave me the answer key to the test.**

12. Change this declarative sentence to an exclamatory sentence.
    **In the fourth inning, Johnny Bench hit a grand slam.**

    **Bench hit a grand slam!**

*Kinds of Sentences* • **Challenge**

# ▶Sensory Description

Your senses help you experience the world around you. Details that capture sense impressions are called *sensory details*. Writers use sensory details to re-create the sight, sound, smell, taste, and touch of things.

Before : *I felt hot and tired after the race through the desert.*

Improved: *Every inch of my body ached after the grueling race through the scorching, arid desert.*

1.  Imagine a scene you would like to see outside of a window. Such scenes may include a street scene, a mountain landscape, inner-city life, or your backyard. Next, write a complete, detailed description of the scene on the lines below. State the location of the scene in the first sentence, then use sensory details to make your description as vivid as possible.

_____

_____

_____

_____

_____

_____

_____

_____

_____

_____

_____

**WRITER'S CRAFT**

**COMPREHENSION**

# ▶ Compare and Contrast

Review "S.O.R. Losers" for examples of people whose views on cooperation and competition can be compared and contrasted with Ed Sitrow's views on these subjects. Then write a poem about Ed Sitrow. Use these comparisons and contrasts to create vivid images for your readers and to help them understand his character. Ask your teacher about sharing your finished poem with the class. **Answers will vary.**

_____

_____

_____

_____

_____

_____

_____

_____

_____

_____

_____

_____

_____

_____

_____

_____

*Compare and Contrast* • **Challenge**

**UNIT 1**  Cooperation and Competition • **Lesson 5** *S.O.R. Losers*

# ▶The /u/ Sound

**Pronunciation Strategy**
**Write the correct spelling of the words from the respellings below.**

1. /buz´ ərd/     buzzard

2. /kul´ chər/     culture

3. /yung´ stər/     youngster

4. /mus´ kyə lər]     muscular

5. /nuj/     nudge

6. /luv´ lē/     lovely

7. /jus´ tis/     justice

8. /guv´ ərn/     govern

9. /struk´ chər/     structure

10. /kus´ tə mər/     customer

**SPELLING**

**Meaning Strategy**
**Fill in the blanks with a word with the /u/ sound.**
Answers may vary.

11. If you reach the top of a mountain you have reached its ___summit___.

12. A ___vulture___ is a large bird of prey with dark feathers.

13. A mother sings a ___lullaby___ to her baby.

14. When you have no feeling in your foot, it is ___numb___.

15. A sudden, strong rush of wind or air is a ___gust___.

# ▶ Using the Thesaurus

**VOCABULARY**

**The following paragraphs contain some words that are used too often. To make the paragraphs livelier, replace the underlined words with synonyms. Write each synonym on the line after the underlined word. Use your thesaurus to help you.** Answers may vary.

1. A volcano is a landform <u>made from</u> _created by_ the Possible answers shown.

   eruption of liquid rock from under Earth's crust. Molten

   rock can force its way to the surface and erupt as lava.

   Some lava <u>moves</u> _flows_ almost like water and can

   cover large areas before it cools and hardens.

2. Even as a mountain is first forming, the wind and weather

   begin to change it. As hundreds or thousands of years pass,

   the surface wears away, slowly <u>changing</u> _altering_

   the mountain's appearance.

3. Earthquakes can be measured by scientists. One <u>good</u>

   _useful_ instrument is a seismograph. Earthquake

   waves, called seismic waves, move through rocks beneath

   Earth's surface. Seismic waves <u>cause</u> _force_ the

   rocks of Earth's crust to vibrate.

4. Earth has many different types of land. There are hot,

   sandy deserts and cold, frozen tundras. There are thick

   forests, <u>huge</u> _massive_ mountains, and <u>high</u>

   _towering_ plateaus.

*Using the Thesaurus* • Challenge

**UNIT I**  Cooperation and Competition • **Lesson 5** *S.O.R. Losers*

# ▶ Subjects and Predicates

**Underline the groups of words that do not contain both a subject and a predicate.**

Toshi and I walked to school together every morning. <u>Go through the park and across the river.</u> Then we turned left and walked past the post office. Mrs. Rivera, who was in charge of running the post office, always waved to us. <u>At the door to the school, the principal, Mr. Hawkins.</u> Out of breath, we ran through the door. <u>Just in time for our first class, which was Spanish.</u>

My cat Toby is a real character. <u>Always making me laugh.</u> He loves to play. <u>Chasing his toy mouse around the floor.</u> Toby wakes me up every morning. He jumps on my bed and meows softly. <u>Some mornings.</u> I don't want to get up. Toby meows louder and louder. <u>After breakfast.</u> Toby and I are ready for another great day.

**Write a paragraph describing a time when you, or someone you know, competed for a prize or an honor. Make sure you use complete sentences.**

**Answers will vary.**

_____

_____

_____

_____

_____

_____

_____

_____

**GRAMMAR AND USAGE**

# ►Time and Order Words

**WRITER'S CRAFT**

Time order is used to explain the order in which events occur. Words that show time order include *first, next, tomorrow,* and so on.

Place order is used in descriptions to help guide the reader. Words that help the reader move through this type of paragraph include *to the right of, facing the back, to my left.*

1. To practice using chronological order, write a paragraph about your morning routine. After you've written it, mark those words that indicate the time order.
   **Answers will vary.**

   _____

   _____

   _____

   _____

2. Using your imagination or a picture from a book or magazine, write a description using place order.
   **Answers will vary.**

   _____

   _____

   _____

   _____

   _____

   _____

   _____

# ▶Author's Purpose

Write a brief news article for the school paper about the
Fagervik children. Think about what your purpose is for
writing about the children. Is it to inform, explain, entertain,
or persuade? The following are some helpful hints for writing
a good news article. **Answers will vary.**

> ▶ Use a **title** that captures the reader's interest and tells the main idea of the story.
>
> ▶ Think of an interesting and informative lead. A **lead** is the first sentence of a news story, and it tells *who, what, when, where,* and *why.*
>
> ▶ Give your story an angle. An **angle** is the viewpoint, or perspective, from which a story is written.

_____

_____

_____

_____

_____

_____

_____

_____

_____

_____

COMPREHENSION

# ▶ The Short-Vowel Sounds

**SPELLING**

**Pronunciation Strategy**
Write the short-vowel sounds in the words below.

1. accent    /a/, /e/
2. contact   /o/, /a/
3. backward  /a/
4. chemist   /e/, /i/
5. entry     /e/
6. forgot    /o/
7. publish   /u/, /i/
8. imitate   /i/, /i/
9. unfriendly /u/, /e/
10. forgive  /i/

**Rhyming Strategy**
Write a word that rhymes with each word below.

11. jealous   zealous
12. mention   pension, tension
13. number    slumber, lumber
14. sauce     boss, loss, moss, toss

# Word Mapping

Make a word map for the word *government*. Write words under each category.

Answers will vary. Sample answers are shown.

**VOCABULARY**

### People

president, Congress, senator, lawmakers, representative, mayor, judge, governor, cabinet, emperor, legislator, parliament

### Descriptions

official, corrupt, just, legitimate, responsible, free, fair, authoritative, partisan

**government**

### Things/Actions

census, laws, import, export, immigration, inauguration, proclamation, budget, Constitution, declaration, department, trade, tax

### Ideas

authority, empire, dictatorship, monarchy, federalism, liberty, tyranny, patriotism, responsibility, community, freedom, politics, republic

# ► Review

**GRAMMAR AND USAGE**

► **Correct this paragraph changing the mistakes in plurals, pronouns, end punctuation, and capital letters at the beginnings of sentences.**

**my family and I**

Last summer me and my family went to Mackinaw

**We**        **We**

City. us stayed at a bed and breakfast. we rode the ferry

**There**      **ferries**

to Mackinac Island. their were three ferrys from which

**Dad and I**

to choose. i and dad chose the fastest one, but Mom

**my**           **On**

and me sisters didn't really want that. on the island we

visited forts, a fudge shop, and rode a horse-drawn

**That**     **we**

carriage around the island. that night us stayed at the

**One man**          **us**

Grand Hotel. one men at the desk gave them a really

**The**        **my sister and I**

nice room. the next morning me and my sister didn't

want to go home, but we did.

► **Underline all the verbs in this sentence.**

Greg <u>enjoyed</u> walking along the city sidewalks

during his lunch hour. His friend Kim <u>preferred</u> sitting

in the park. Today it <u>was</u> <u>raining</u>. Kim <u>did</u> not <u>want</u> to

sit in the rain. They <u>decided</u> to have lunch in a diner.

Greg always <u>ordered</u> the same meal. He <u>had</u> a tuna

sandwich and a glass of milk. Kim <u>thought</u> his meal

<u>would taste</u> good. She <u>ordered</u> the same meal. By the

time they <u>finished</u>, the rain <u>had stopped</u>.

# Presentation

Presentation refers to the look of your piece of writing. Charts, graphs, illustrations, and photos are all excellent visual aids. You may also wish to add bullets, italics, or underlining to call attention to important points in your text.

**1.** Use the remainder of this page to create a poster advertising a fictional event. Include the name of the event, and the location, date, and time the event is to be held. Be creative with your text and add interest to your poster by including design elements.

**WRITER'S CRAFT**

**UNIT 2** Astronomy • **Lesson I** *Galileo*

# ▶The /ā/ Sound

**Meaning Strategy**
**Complete each sentence with a single-syllable word that uses the /ā/ sound.**    Answers will vary.

1. Queen Victoria's __reign_____ lasted from 1837 to 1901.

2. Blood flows through your body through __veins_____ and arteries.

3. The massive truck __weighed_____ almost four tons.

4. If you're traveling to another country, it's important to know the exchange __rate_____ before you leave.

5. We had to __pay_____ for our meal before leaving the restaurant.

6. The seal was so tight that not even a __blade_____ of grass would slip through it.

7. The trees provided __shade_____ from the sunshine.

8. In order to stay in good __shape_____, I exercise everyday and eat healthful food.

9. My favorite sweatshirt is so old that the ends are starting to __fray_____.

10. We put the painting into a picture __frame_____.

*The /ā/ Sound* • Challenge

# ▶Science Words

**Read the paragraph on biology, and then define the science words that are underlined in the paragraph.**

Biology is a science that studies life and living organisms. It attempts to explain the origin and function of all that is living. Botany and zoology are different branches of biology. If you study biology you will learn about many different ecosystems. You will also learn about viruses, mutations, and photosynthesis, and how they influence living organisms.

1. organisms: a living animal or plant having organs that function together to maintain vital activities

2. botany: the science or study of plants

3. zoology: the science that deals with animal life

4. ecosystems: a group of living organisms and their environment

5. viruses: any of a group of disease-causing microorganisms

6. mutations: a sudden change in a gene or chromosome that affects the form or quality of offspring

**VOCABULARY**

**MECHANICS**

# ▶Capitalization: Places

▶ **Underline the letters that should be capitalized. Draw a slash through letters that should not be capital letters.**

On <u>m</u>emorial <u>d</u>ay, <u>m</u>onday, <u>m</u>ay 30, president <u>c</u>linton began his V̶isit to eastern C̶ities. On <u>t</u>uesday, he sailed down the <u>h</u>udson <u>r</u>iver to <u>n</u>ew <u>y</u>ork <u>c</u>ity. <u>w</u>ednesday, he and <u>m</u>rs. <u>c</u>linton flew A̶cross <u>n</u>ew <u>j</u>ersey and the <u>d</u>elaware <u>r</u>iver to <u>p</u>hiladelphia. After visiting <u>c</u>hester <u>c</u>ounty, the <u>c</u>lintons went into the <u>a</u>ppalachian <u>m</u>ountains for a R̶ally in <u>h</u>arrisburg.

▶ **Write a paragraph that includes at least eight of the following ten capitalization rules: countries, cities, states, counties, bodies of water, mountains, months, days, holidays, and people's titles.**  Answers will vary.

_____

_____

_____

_____

_____

_____

_____

_____

_____

**UNIT 2** Astronomy • **Lesson I** *Galileo*

# Organizing by Order

**Order of importance is a way to develop and organize
the paragraphs you write.**

1. Read the following paragraph then write the points in the paragraph ranging from most important to least important on the lines provided.

   Walking several miles a day has recently become an important part of my daily schedule. The most important reason I have for starting to walk this distance every day is that walking is good aerobic exercise. In addition, my doctor tells me that walking will help to keep my circulation in good condition. Another important point is that I have wanted to set a goal for myself and discipline myself until I have reached that goal. I began walking a quarter of a mile (about 0.40 km) daily and gradually increased the mileage. But perhaps I walk every day simply because I enjoy walking. I can walk by myself and take delight in the scenery, or I can walk with friends and enjoy their company.

   1. most important ___Walking is good aerobic exercise.___

   2. important ___I want to set and meet a goal.___

   3. least important ___I enjoy walking.___

2. Practice using order of importance by writing a paragraph describing your possessions. These possessions may be personal possessions or belong to your entire family. They may be things that are old and things that are new.

   _____

   _____

   _____

   _____

   _____

WRITER'S CRAFT

**UNIT 2**  Astronomy • **Lesson I** *Galileo*

# ▶ Place and Location Words

**WRITER'S CRAFT**

Place and location words are descriptors that help
readers move through a piece of writing. Taking care
to order the details in your writing by using place and
location words can allow readers to visualize your
descriptions.

1.  Select a photograph from a book or magazine and
write a description of the photograph using place and
location words.

_____

_____

_____

_____

_____

_____

2. Write a description using all of the following place and
location words and phrases. You may use them in any order.

| across<br>in front of | beside<br>to the left of | behind<br>to the far right of |
| --- | --- | --- |

_____

_____

_____

_____

# ▶The /ē/ Sound

**Meaning Strategy**
**Complete the sentences with a single-syllable word that uses the /ē/ sound.** Answers may vary.

1. The __fleet__ of ships sailed past the harbor and out into the ocean.

2. Our teacher asked us to write a paper focused on one topic, or __theme__.

3. It's natural to __grieve__ the loss of a loved one.

4. The suspect would __plead__ guilty to the charges.

5. After the Civil War, slaves became __free__.

6. I must have short arms because the __sleeves__ on my shirt are too long.

7. A cool __breeze__ feels nice on a hot, sunny day.

8. President Franklin D. Roosevelt said, "The only thing we have to __fear__ is __fear__ itself."

9. I love to go fly-fishing in a mountain __stream__.

10. A secret, devious, or underhanded plot is known as a __scheme__.

**SPELLING**

# ▶ Greek Roots

Greek roots are listed in the box. Below the box are
definitions for each root and an example of a word using
the root. Match the root with the definition and write
your own example. The first one is done for you.

**Answers
will vary.**

| | | | |
|---|---|---|---|
| cracy | mono | crit | poly |
| hypno | thermo | polis | scopos |

**1.** type of government; <u>democracy</u>

**cracy** _____ **theocracy** _____

**2.** to judge; <u>critique</u>

**crit** _____ **critic** _____

**3.** one; <u>monopoly</u>

**mono** _____ **monocle** _____

**4.** spy, watcher; <u>microscope</u>

**scopos** _____ **telescope** _____

**5.** more than one; <u>polygon</u>

**poly** _____ **polyglot** _____

**6.** heat; <u>thermometer</u>

**thermo** _____ **thermos** _____

**7.** city; <u>police</u>

**polis** _____ **politician** _____

**8.** sleep; <u>hypnotic</u>

**hypno** _____ **hypnosis** _____

**VOCABULARY**

Name _____ Date _____

 # Capitalization: Titles

▶ **Underline the letters that should be capitalized in the following paragraph.**

    For my english class, I am writing a research paper about the depression. In the school library, I found two books, *no promises in the wind* and *the grapes of wrath*, but they were fiction and not of much use. At the university library, I searched the *new york times*, the *cleveland plain dealer*, *illustrated american history*, and *cobblestone*. There were several articles which helped me write my paper.

▶ **Write a sentence for each of the following.**   **Answers will vary.**

   **1.** proper adjective _____

   **2.** book title _____

   **3.** movie title _____

   **4.** magazine title _____

   **5.** newspaper title _____

   **6.** historic event _____

   **7.** religion _____

   **8.** language _____

   **9.** ethnic group _____

**MECHANICS**

**UNIT 2**  Astronomy • **Lesson 2** *Telescopes*

# ▶Comparing and Contrasting

**WRITER'S CRAFT**

▶**You can use comparison to help define two similar objects. Choose two of the following pairs to compare. List at least three similarities between the objects in each pair.**

Chinese and Italian food      running and walking
TV and movies      kickball and soccer
the East Coast and the West Coast      tennis and badminton
tragedy and comedy

    Answers will vary.

_____

_____

_____

▶**You can explain or describe something by contrasting it with its opposite. Choose two of the above pairs to contrast. Tell three ways in which they are different.**

    Answers will vary.

_____

_____

_____

▶**Choose one pair that you compared or contrasted. Write a paragraph that more thoroughly explains the pair's likenesses or differences.**

    Answers will vary.

_____

_____

_____

_____

_____

# ▶The /ē/ Sound

**Meaning Strategy**
**Complete the sentences with a one-syllable word that uses the /ē/ sound.** Answers will vary.

1. An automobile has to yield _____ the right of way to pedestrians in a crosswalk.

2. After scoring four runs in the fifth inning, the team took to the
   field _____ with confidence.

3. My Aunt Gertrude has four nephews and one niece _____.

4. To cede _____ territory is to give up possession or to surrender.

5. I have to remember to bring my fishing reel _____ when we go to the lake this summer.

**Pronunciation Strategy**
**Write the spelling of the word based on the phonetic pronunciation.**

6. /lē′ nē ənt/    lenient _____

7. /bi lēv′/    believe _____

8. /pās′ trē/    pastry _____

9. /fung′ kē/    funky _____

10. /mə shēn′/    machine _____

SPELLING

# ▶ Homographs

**VOCABULARY**

**The following pairs of words are homographs. Write a definition for each word as a noun and as a verb. Then use each in a sentence.**

**1.** console (noun) cabinet _____

    sentence:   Answers will vary. _____

_____

**2.** console (verb) to ease grief _____

    sentence:   Answers will vary. _____

_____

**3.** rose (noun)   a flower _____

    sentence:   Answers will vary. _____

_____

**4.** rose (verb)   the past tense of rise _____

    sentence:   Answers will vary. _____

_____

**5.** dove (noun)   a small or medium size bird of the pigeon

family _____

    sentence:   Answers will vary. _____

**6.** dove (verb)   the past tense of dive _____

    sentence:   Answers will vary. _____

_____

# Abbreviations

▶ **Write the abbreviations for the following words.**

1. page _p._____          6. pages _pp._____

2. December _Dec._____     7. Wednesday _Wed._____

3. street _St._____        8. kilometer _km_____

4. feet _ft._____          9. post meridiem _P.M._____

5. Random Access            10. Eastern Standard Time
   Memory _RAM_____           _EST_____

▶ **Write as many abbreviations as you can think of and the word each one stands for in the categories listed. Some sample answers have been provided to help you begin your list.**

| Time and Direction | Measurement | Miscellaneous |
|---|---|---|
| SW, southwest | tbsp., tablespoon | AKA, also known as |
| NE, Northeast | tsp., teaspoon | etc., et cetera |
| EST, Eastern StandardTime | kg, Kilogram | WWW, World Wide Web |
| | | |
| | | |
| | | |
| | | |

MECHANICS

**WRITER'S CRAFT**

# ▶ Aim/Purpose/Audience

▶ Suppose that you are writing about a person who has been important in your life. You are asked to describe why that person has affected you so strongly. Write three different topic sentences for three different audiences (friends, classmates, readers of a newspaper, family member and so on) using any primary purpose such as to entertain, describe, inform, or explain. In thinking about your audience and purpose try to be sensitive to their background, values, and your relationship with them.

Who is audience #1? _____

What do you want to achieve? _____

_____

Topic sentence for audience one. _____

_____

Who is audience #2? _____

What do you want to achieve? _____

_____

Topic sentence for audience two. _____

_____

Who is audience #3? _____

What do you want to achieve? _____

_____

Topic sentence for audience three. _____

_____

# Main Idea and Details

▶ Imagine that you are the book reviewer for a newspaper. Your job is to write a review of the new article that you have just read: "Circles, Squares, and Daggers: How Native Americans Watched the Skies." The first part of your review must include a summary of the article. You can do this summary by writing a paragraph that begins with a main idea sentence followed by supporting detail sentences. The second part of your review must include your opinions about the article.

▶ Below, write a draft of the summary portion of your review. Then, on a separate sheet of paper, write your entire review for the newspaper.

Answers will vary.

_____

_____

_____

_____

_____

_____

_____

_____

_____

_____

**COMPREHENSION**

# ▶The /ō/ Sound

**SPELLING**

### Meaning Strategy
**Complete the sentences with a one-syllable word that uses the /ō/ sound.** Answers may vary.

1. If you're going to use someone else's words, you should ___quote___ the author.

2. The king was sitting on his ___throne___ when he received the bad news.

3. We decided to stop paddling and just ___float___ down the stream.

4. At first I thought Anna had an unusual sense of humor, but lately I think it's ___grown___ on me.

5. I would like to ___hone___, or sharpen, my writing skills this year.

6. I know the ending of the story because I ___wrote___ it.

7. I can't wait for the first snowfall so I can grab my skis and hit the ___slopes___.

8. William is such a klutz. He's the most accident ___prone___ person I know.

9. The professor didn't know the answer because it was outside his ___scope___ of expertise.

10. I am lucky because I have many friends but few ___foes___.

# Latin Roots

Latin roots are listed in the box. Below the box are definitions for each root and an example of a word using the root. Match the root with the definition and write your own example. The first one is done for you.

**Answers will vary.**

| civis | crimen | dens | firmare |
|-------|--------|------|---------|
| juvenis | fumus | mecari | mare |

1. young; <u>rejuvenate</u>

 **juvenis** _____  juvenile _____

2. tooth; <u>dentist</u>

 dens _____  dentistry _____

3. crime; <u>criminal</u>

 crimen _____  criminology _____

4. make firm; <u>affirm</u>

 firmare _____  firmament _____

5. citizen; <u>civilization</u>

 civis _____  civility _____

6. market; <u>merchant</u>

 mecari _____  mercantile _____

7. sea; <u>marine</u>

 mare _____  mariner _____

8. smoke; <u>fume</u>

 fumus _____  fumigate _____

**VOCABULARY**

**MECHANICS**

# ▶ Commas in Places and Dates

**Use comma rules in the following examples.**    Answers will vary.

1. Create a heading for a business letter.

   _____

   _____

   _____

2. Create an inside address for a business letter.

   _____

   _____

   _____

3. Use your birthdate in a sentence; include the day of the week, the month, the day date, and the year.

   _____

   _____

4. Use your address in a sentence; include street address, city, state, and zip code.

   _____

   _____

5. Use a European city and country in a sentence.

   _____

   _____

# ▶ Supporting Details

**Every main point you make in your writing should be supported with facts, quotations, examples or descriptions.**

**1.** Choose one of these topics about which to write a paragraph.

   ▶ A person who makes me laugh

   ▶ A place I (love, hate) to be

   ▶ My (most, least) favorite possession

**On the lines below, list at least ten details about the topic you have chosen. You may use facts, quotations, examples, descriptions, or a combination of these.**

_____

_____

_____

_____

_____

_____

_____

_____

_____

_____

**WRITER'S CRAFT**

# The /ī/ Sound

**Meaning Strategy**
**Complete the sentences with a one-syllable word that uses the /ī/ sound.**    **Answers may vary.**

1. It's a good idea to arrive at the airport at least an hour before your
   **flight** _____.

2. When Tom let out a long, deep **sigh** _____ , I knew he was tired and ready to go home.

3. My pet rabbit is often timid and **shy** _____ in front of strangers.

4. I wasn't allowed to get my driver's license until I knew how to change a flat **tire** _____.

5. The eagle spread out his wings and seemed to effortlessly
   **glide** _____ onto the top of the tree.

6. It is important to always **cite** _____ your sources when you write a paper.

7. I like to take long **hikes** _____ through nature trails during the summer.

8. My cousin Lu Chan is so smart. He's always coming up with
   **bright** _____ ideas.

9. The score was **tied** _____ five to five when the game was over.

10. I always **shine** _____ my shoes before special occasions.

SPELLING

# ▶ Prefixes

▶ The following words share the common Latin prefix *circum-*. Write definitions of the words. Use a dictionary if necessary.

1. circumnavigate _sail completely around_

2. circumference _line bounding any rounded plane figure_

3. circumstance _state of affairs surrounding a person, etc._

4. What do you think the Latin prefix *circum-* means? _around_

▶ The following words share the common prefix *pre-*. Write definitions of the words. Use a dictionary if necessary.

5. precook _to cook beforehand_

6. predict _to announce beforehand_

7. preempt _to get or take possession before others_

8. What do you think the prefix *pre-* means? _before_

▶ The following words share the common prefix *con-*. Write definitions of the words. Use a dictionary if necessary.

9. concur _to hold the same opinion_

10. concurrent _existing or happening at the same time_

11. concord _an agreement between persons, nations, etc._

12. What do you think the prefix *con-* means? _together or with_

**VOCABULARY**

Challenge • *Prefixes*

**MECHANICS**

# ▶ Parentheses, Hyphens, Dashes, and Ellipses

**Write sentences using the following instructions.**

**Answers will vary.**

1. Show the correct use of parentheses in a sentence telling what you did last night.

_____

2. Use a hyphen to create an adjective describing the ocean.

_____

3. Use a hyphen to correctly divide a word into syllables at the end of a line.

_____

_____

4. Use a dash to show a sudden break in thought or speech concerning your grades.

_____

5. Use an ellipses to partially quote a friend's statement about the weather.

_____

6. Use a hyphen correctly in a number indicating the age of your grandmother.

_____

# Taking Notes

**After locating appropriate sources, read and take notes on pertinent information. Note taking involves summarizing, quoting directly, and paraphrasing. Summarize by focusing on key points and concepts. Use direct quotations when the author has explained an idea or stated an opinion especially well. Paraphrase by writing the information in your own words.**

1. Choose a topic that interests you from those listed below. Gather some sources of information about the topic. Write the name of your topic on the first line below. For example, if you have chosen "a favorite food," you might write the name of that particular food. Then write notes about the topic on the remaining lines. Include each of the three note taking techniques.

   Possible topics: *a favorite hobby, an historical figure, a favorite food, a favorite sport, fashion or costumes, movies, airplanes.*

   _____

   _____

   _____

   _____

   _____

   _____

   _____

   _____

   _____

**WRITER'S CRAFT**

**UNIT 2** Astronomy • **Lesson 5** *The Mystery of Mars*

# ▶ Bibliography/Citations

**WRITER'S CRAFT**

1. Find examples of bibliographies in other books that are available in your classroom library. Answer the following questions based on those bibliographies. **Answers will vary.**

   **a.** Write the title of a book, the date of publication of that book, and the publisher's name.

   _____

   **b.** Give the name of a magazine, the title of the article in that magazine, the volume of the magazine, the date the article was published, and the page numbers.

   _____

2. Use the lines provided to write a bibliography using the following sources.

   **a.** Jonathan Dillard wrote the magazine article "The Computer Grapevine" which appeared in *Computer Magazine* on page 121 of the February 2000 issue.

   **b.** Lawrence Quigley wrote the book *Elementary Computer Graphics.* It was published by Franklin Publishing Company in Franklin, Virginia, in 1999.

   **c.** Ralph Epstein wrote an article titled "Computer" for the 1999 edition of *The World Book Encyclopedia*, Vol. 4, pp. 740-746.

   Dillard, Jonathan. "The Computer Grapevine." *Computer*

   *Magazine,* February 2000, p. 121.

   Epstein, Ralph. "Computer." *The World Book Encyclopedia,*

   Vol. 4 (1999), pp. 740–746.

   Quigley, Lawrence. *Elementary Computer Graphics.*

   Franklin, Virginia: Franklin Publishing Company, 1999.

**UNIT 2** Astronomy • **Lesson 6** *Stars*

# ▶ Classifying and Categorizing

Use a card or computer catalog to conduct a search on the key word *stars*. Classify the information that your search yields into categories. For example, you will likely have a category for information on stars in the sky and another for information on movie stars. List these and other categories you find. Then think of ways to further classify information in the categories. For example, movie stars could be further classified as male, female, child and adult.

Finally, create a chart that illustrates that you classified and categorized the information you found. Draw your chart in the space below.

**Answers will vary.**

Name _____ Date _____

**UNIT 2** Astronomy • **Lesson 6** *Stars*

# ▶The /o͞o/ and /ū/ Sounds

**Meaning Strategy**
**Complete the sentences with a word that uses the /o͞o/
or /ū/ sound.** Answers may vary.

SPELLING

1. The part of a plant that anchors it and stores food is called the
   __root__.

2. In a __lunar__ eclipse, Earth moves between the sun and
   the moon, blocking the sun's rays from the moon.

3. Have you received the latest __issue__ of the newspaper?

4. A __mushroom__ is a fungus that is often shaped like an umbrella.

5. She __stooped__ to pick up the paper she had dropped.

6. Something that is not ordinary or common is __unusual__.

7. The planet __Pluto__ is farthest away from the sun.

8. Something that is true everywhere or exists everywhere is known as
   __universal__.

9. A __cube__ has six equal, square faces.

10. No one knows for sure what is going to happen in the
    __future__.

**54** **UNIT 2 • Lesson 6**                    *The /o͞o/ and /ū/ Sounds* • **Challenge**

# Suffixes

▶ The following words share the common suffix *-able*. Write definitions of the words. Use a dictionary if necessary.

1. expandable _able to make larger, or expand_

2. expendable _able to be expended; may be sacrificed_

3. dependable _can be depended upon_

4. What do you think the suffix *-able* means? _capable or able_

▶ Add the suffix *-able* to two words of your own.

5. _Answers will vary._

6. _Answers will vary._

▶ The following words share the common suffix *-less*. Write definitions of the words. Use a dictionary if necessary.

7. sunless _without sun_

8. homeless _without a home_

9. shameless _without shame_

10. What do you think the suffix *-less* means? _without_

▶ Add the suffix *-less* to two words of your own.

11. _Answers will vary._

12. _Answers will vary._

**VOCABULARY**

**MECHANICS**

# Quotations, Underlining, and Apostrophes

**Edit the following dialogue. Add quotation marks, underlining and apostrophes when needed. Be sure to use a new paragraph for each new speaker.**

Last weekend, Brittany and Trish went to an amusement park they read about in an article in the magazine Ranger Rick. "I'm so glad you asked me to come to the park with you," Brittany said. "Let's go ride [new paragraph] the roller coaster before the line becomes too long," Trish replied. Brittany exclaimed, "Wow! That's the best [new paragraph] coaster I've ever ridden." "We should go have some of that ice cream that my brother's company supplies," Trish suggested. "Then I want to ride the Giant Wheel." "Is it time for your dad to pick us up, or do we have [new paragraph] more time to ride?" Brittany asked. "He's coming at four, so we have time for one more ride," Trish answered.

"This is the most fun we've had all summer."

# Exact Words

1. Words like *said* and *very* are often overused. Replace them with more exact words. For instance, *very pretty = beautiful.*

   Very angry = <u>irate</u>          very thin = <u>gaunt</u>

   Answers may vary from those shown

   Dad said in a loud voice, "Come in here." <u>shouted</u>

   The villain said, "Get down." <u>demanded</u>

   "You will have your money for team uniforms," said the principal.

   <u>pledged</u>

   "Wha-a-t  h-h-appened?" said the frightened boy.

   <u>stammered</u>

2. Underline the most appropriate word from the pair given in parentheses.

   **a.** The teacher (<u>praised</u>, *eulogized*) the class for its good work on the project.

   **b.** The lifeguard's (<u>skin</u>, *hide*) was dry from overexposure to the sun.

   **c.** The children (<u>donated</u>, *bestowed*) their time to help restore the damage to the building.

   **d.** The dictator was (*conquered*, <u>overthrown</u>) by his own brother.

3. The following words are similar, but not equally appropriate in every situation. Check the precise meaning of each word, and then use each in a sentence. Check all words before writing your sentences.

   *droll*    <u>The coach had a droll sense of humor.</u>

   *comical*  <u>The clowns in the circus were truly comical.</u>

WRITER'S CRAFT

**UNIT 2** Astronomy • **Lesson 7** *The Book that Saved the Earth*

# The Long-Vowel Sounds

SPELLING

**Proofreading Strategy**

**Proofread the following paragraphs. Cross out any words that are misspelled and write the correct spelling above the word.**

Heredity is the transfer of ~~trates~~ **traits** from one ~~generaition~~ **generation** to the next. ~~Theese~~ **These** traits are passed through chromosomes.

~~Scentists~~ **Scientists** have ~~knoawn~~ **known** for years that chemicals exist on all ~~chromoseames~~ **chromosomes**. The ~~moleculyle~~ **molecule** DNA, or deoxyribonucleic acid, stores the ~~coaded informaition~~ **coded information** that determines the traits of a living thing. All living things have DNA. However, the code, or the order in which the DNA chemicals ~~appeer~~ **appear**, is different for different organisms.

A ~~gean~~ **gene** is a ~~greup~~ **group** of DNA chemicals on a chromosome.

Each gene controls one or more traits. The genes control the traits because they control which ~~proteens~~ **proteins** the cell makes.

Genes don't determine ~~everithing~~ **everything** about an organism's appearance. The ~~envyronment~~ **environment** also helps determine appearances. For example, genes ~~maye~~ **may** determine the tallest we can be, but diet and health will help determine our actual ~~heit~~ **height**.

*The Long-Vowel Sounds* • **Challenge**

# ▶Review

It is easier to learn new words if you can break them down into smaller parts. Once you know what each part or syllable means, you can put them together to define the word. Write definitions of the words using the Greek roots given in the box.

> *micro* = small   *poly* = many   *bi, bio* = life   *log, ology* = to speak
> *hydr* = water   *geo* = earth   *phobia* = fear   *tele* = far off
> *gon* = having angles

1. biology: the study of living things; i.e. to speak about living things

2. microbiology: the study of very small living organisms; i.e. to speak about small living things

3. hydrology: the study of water; i.e. to speak about water

4. geology: the study of the earth; i.e. to speak about the earth

5. hydrophobia: an abnormal fear of water

6. telecommunicate: to communicate from far away locations

7. geoscience: earth  science

8. polygon: a figure having three or more sides

**VOCABULARY**

Name _____ Date _____

**MECHANICS**

# ▶Review

1. Write a dialogue between you and a friend about the latest books and stories you have read.

   **Answers will vary.**

   _____

   _____

   _____

   _____

2. Write a short paragraph about your state including names of a park, a river, a city, a holiday, and using a proper adjective.

   _____

   _____

   _____

3. Write a sentence using an ellipsis.

   _____

4. Write a sentence using dashes.

   _____

5. Write a sentence using parentheses.

   _____

6. Write a sentence that includes a hyphen, a contraction, and a possessive noun.

   _____

*Review* • Challenge

**UNIT 2**   Astronomy • **Lesson 7** *The Book that Saved the Earth*

# ▶ Plot

**The chain of events in a story is called the *plot*. The plot introduces a problem and follows the characters as they solve it. On the lines below, summarize a story you have recently read. Include all the elements of a plot.**

Students should tell about a problem the characters had

in the beginning. In the middle, the students should

explain how the characters struggled with the problem.

They should also include the climax and how the problem

was resolved. The conclusion finishes telling how the

problem is solved.

_____

_____

_____

_____

_____

_____

_____

_____

_____

_____

**WRITER'S CRAFT**

# ▶ Written with Purpose

**COMPREHENSION**

Everything that's written is written for a reason, or with a purpose. We encounter or use written messages in our daily lives, but we often do not think about why they were written. Sometimes people who write text or messages have more than one purpose for writing. Below is an example. This message appeared on a hardware store sign. Read the sign carefully, and explain below why the purpose of this message could be to inform, explain, entertain, **and** persuade.

```
┌─────────────────────────────┐
│      HANDY HARDWARE         │
│  We Happen to Have It All!  │
├─────────────────────────────┤
│         Pesticide,          │
├─────────────────────────────┤
│       Bones, Rawhide,       │
├─────────────────────────────┤
│     Bargains Bonafide,      │
├─────────────────────────────┤
│        Come Inside!         │
└─────────────────────────────┘
```

Answers will vary. Possible answers are shown.

To inform: The ad tells what kind of store it is and that the store has a variety of things inside.

To explain: The ad explains some of the things customers will find inside the store.

To entertain: The ad uses funny and clever language, including alliteration and rhyme to capture people's attention.

To persuade: It is an advertisement. Ads are created to persuade people to do something—to take a look or to buy.

# ▶ The /ow/ Sound

**Pronunciation Strategy** Write a synonym that has the /ow/ sound for each word or group of words. **Answers may vary.**

1. mighty     powerful
2. sofa     couch
3. sleepy     drowsy
4. pants     trousers
5. loud, wailing cry     howl
6. set of clothes     outfit
7. to be uncertain about     doubt
8. lacking style in dress     dowdy
9. long table     counter
10. disorderly     rowdy

**SPELLING**

**Answers will vary.**

**Rhyming Strategy** Write two words with the /ow/ sound that rhyme with each word below. **Sample answers shown.**

| | | |
|---|---|---|
| 11. bounce | counts | pounce |
| 12. flower | tower | sour |
| 13. slouch | couch | pouch |
| 14. pound | bound | round |
| 15. down | crown | noun |

# ▶ Context Clues

> Writers give context clues in five main ways:
>
> **Definition**—The meaning of the word is stated.
>
> **Example**—The meaning of the unfamiliar word is explained through examples.
>
> **Comparison**—The unfamiliar word is similar to a familiar word or phrase.
>
> **Contrast**—The unfamiliar word is opposite a familiar word or phrase.
>
> **Cause and Effect**—The unfamiliar word is explained as part of a cause-and-effect relationship.

**Match the type of context clue with the sentence in which it is used. Write the meaning of the underlined word using context clues.**

    **a.** definition    **b.** example    **c.** comparison

    **d.** contrast    **e.** cause and effect

**1.** __c__ Why would I <u>retract</u> my statement? I don't want to withdraw it.

*Retract* means __withdraw_____

**2.** __e__ I know I looked <u>perplexed</u> because his arguments always leave me puzzled.

*Perplexed* means __puzzled_____

**3.** __a__ China's Hwang-ho River flooded in 1931, causing a <u>calamity</u>, or disaster.

*Calamity* means __disaster_____

                *Context Clues* • **Challenge**

# ▶ Adjectives

**Fill in the blank with appropriate adjectives, including articles.**

Answers will vary.

1. _____ _____ box contains all of my

   _____ presents.

2. He drove down the _____ road until he came

   to _____ _____ farm.

3. One of _____ days, my _____ brother will

   understand how to clean his _____ dog.

4. Chop _____ head of cabbage, _____

   carrots, and _____ _____ onion.

5. Place _____ vegetables in _____

   _____ pot.

6. Reduce _____ heat, and add _____ cans of

   _____ tomatoes.

7. The _____ door creaked as Suzy opened it.

8. _____ light was _____, but she could see

   _____ cobwebs covered _____

   _____ furniture.

9. She approached _____ _____ trunk hoping

   to find _____ _____ doll quickly.

10. Finally we reached _____ _____ corner and

    walked on to our _____ home.

**GRAMMAR AND USAGE**

► # Organization of a Descriptive Paragraph

**WRITER'S CRAFT**

Descriptive writing is like taking a picture. To do each effectively, you must first find a focus. State the focus in the topic sentence. Details appealing to the reader's senses are organized in a way that makes sense such as from *front to back, top to bottom, far to near, left to right, most recent to least.* You can use similes and metaphors along with concrete nouns, adjectives, and adverbs to make the description vivid and realistic.

**Write a five-paragraph essay describing your room at its messiest; the crowd at a concert or sports event, or your most interesting teacher. The first paragraph consists of an introduction. The next three give details about three different aspects of the object, location, or person being described. The final paragraph concludes or summarizes the description. Use an additional sheet of paper to complete your essay.**

Answers will vary.

_____

_____

_____

_____

_____

_____

_____

_____

_____

Name _____ Date _____

 # Compare and Contrast

In 20 years, many things in the world and about you will be different. Complete the chart below to show comparisons and contrasts between your life now and what your life may be like 20 years from now. **Answers will vary.**

Following are some questions you might want to consider when completing the chart.

1. How old will you be?

2. What will schools be like? Will you be in school?

3. What will families be like? What kind of homes will people live in?

4. Will you still eat the same kinds of food? Or, will food be different?

5. What kinds of communication and transportation will there be?

6. Will anything be the same? What things will be the same?

| Life Now | Life in 20 years |
| --- | --- |
| | |

# ► The Final /əl/ Sound

**SPELLING**

**Meaning Strategy** Write a word with the /əl/ sound to replace the underlined words. Answers may vary.

1. Washington, D.C., is the <u>center of government</u> of the United States.
   capital _____

2. On <u>usual</u> days, visitors can see Congress in action. normal _____

3. This jacket is <u>exactly the same as</u> the one I lost last year. identical to _____

4. The <u>representative sign</u> for copyright is ©. symbol _____

5. My <u>mother's brother</u> is coming to visit. uncle _____

6. The two friends had an <u>angry conflict</u> about who would pay for

   dinner. quarrel _____

7. Katharine wrote a <u>short feature</u> about dolphins in the magazine.
   article _____

8. <u>More than two</u> stars were added to the United States flag in the

   twentieth century. Several _____

9. The contract was signed in <u>non-erasable</u> ink. indelible _____

10. The teacher couldn't hear Jason's answer because he <u>spoke almost</u>

    <u>with his mouth closed</u>. mumbled _____

# ▶ Concept Words

**The following passage is about climate. Concept words relating to** *climate* **are underlined.**

Where a region is on Earth determines its climate. Climate is the typical weather pattern in a place over a long period. It includes precipitation, temperature, and seasonal patterns. The average temperature of a region falls as you move away from the equator to higher latitudes.

Next to an ocean or large lake, air blowing inland is moist from the evaporated water. Because of this, coastal areas typically have more humidity than inland areas. Climate is one of several nonliving factors that affect the environment.

**Write the meaning of the underlined words below. Use a dictionary to help you if necessary.**

1. region: a geographic area having one or more unifying characteristics

2. precipitation: any form of water, such as rain, hail, or snow, that falls to Earth

3. latitudes: the distance north or south of the equator

4. evaporated: changed from a solid or liquid into a gas

5. humidity: moistness or dampness of the atmosphere

6. environment: the conditions in which all inhabitants of Earth live; the land, air, and water

**VOCABULARY**

# Adverbs

**GRAMMAR AND USAGE**

▶ **Rewrite these sentences adding at least one adverb to each one.**

**Answers may vary.**

1. The car drove down the driveway.

   _____

2. The movie was long and boring.

   _____

3. Finding the lost dog took several hours.

   _____

▶ **Write sentences using the following directions.**

**Answers may vary.**

4. an adverb that tells when

   _____

5. an adverb that tells where

   _____

6. an adverb that tells to what extent

   _____

7. an adverb that tells how

   _____

8. an adverb modifying a verb

   _____

9. an adverb modifying an adjective

   _____

10. an adverb modifying an adverb

    _____

# Transition Words

**Transition words help signal readers to expect information.**

1. Underline the transitional expressions. On the lines below, explain how they effect the paragraph.

   Doctors have many different ways to help people with allergies. Sometimes they give patients a nose spray, or a pill, or an injection. These medicines help stop such allergic reactions as itching, sneezing, coughing or wheezing. Doctors also tell patients to clear their homes of certain pets and allergens such as dust.

   *Sometimes, also.* **Students may comment that they give**
   _____
   **the paragraph cohesiveness.**
   _____

   _____

2. For the topic sentence below, supply three to five relevant details. Then, on the lines below, write a paragraph using the topic sentence and your supporting details. Connect those details with transitional words and expressions.

   Topic Sentence: Raising a child today is very expensive.

   Details: **Answers will vary.** _____

   _____

   _____

   _____

   _____

   _____

   _____

**WRITER'S CRAFT**

# The /or/ and /är/ Sounds

**SPELLING**

**Visualization Strategy** Unscramble the underlined words.
**Each word contains the /or/ or /är/ sound.**

1. "All <u>boarad</u>," said the captain. _____aboard_____

2. We picked apples and strawberries at the <u>crorhad</u>. _____orchard_____

3. The <u>romal</u> of the story is: Those that live in glass houses shouldn't

   throw stones. _____moral_____

4. I threw the stone <u>rhtrefa</u> than my brother. _____farther_____

5. Daniel has seen both dolphins and <u>oispesrop</u> swimming in the ocean.
   _____porpoises_____

6. The top of a compass rose always points <u>rotnh</u>. _____north_____

7. The <u>cursoe</u> of the river is the lake upstream. _____source_____

8. The opposite of the port side of a boat or ship is <u>basortrad</u>.
   _____starboard_____

9. The boats were docked in the <u>barhor</u>. _____harbor_____

10. A caterpillar is the <u>ralva</u> of a butterfly. _____larva_____

# ▶Spanish Words

▶Below are words from foreign languages. Write the words that are from Spanish.

| siesta tornado | grill ballet | cocoa avocado | bracelet tomato | chowder bungalow |
|---|---|---|---|---|

1. siesta _____

2. cocoa _____

3. tornado _____

4. avocado _____

5. tomato _____

▶Answer the following riddles. Each answer is a word from Spanish.

6. I am a large, greenish brown lizard. What am I? __iguana_____

7. I am an insect that sucks the blood of humans and animals and makes them itch. What am I? __mosquito_____

8. I am a deep valley with steep sides. What am I? __canyon_____

9. I am a large aquatic reptile related to the crocodile. What am I? __alligator_____

10. I am a fenced enclosure for cattle or horses. What am I?
__corral_____

**VOCABULARY**

**UNIT 3**   Heritage • **Lesson 3** *The West Side*

# ▶ Prepositions

**Write two poems of your own using the subjects listed below. Try to include one prepositional phrase in each line of each poem.**

Answers will vary

Example:        Rain

Rain on the green grass,

And rain on the tree,

And rain on the housetop,

But not upon me.


Snow

_____

_____

_____

_____


The Sun

_____

_____

_____

_____

# ▶Sensory Details

To affect the reader as strongly as possible a writer tries to evoke a strong response by using vivid images. These images are brought about with *sensory detail*.

▶ **To practice using effective sensory details, circle the most precise words to complete each sentence.**

1. The engine (made an awful sound, (hissed and sputtered) (its objections)).

2. A (wonderful, (spicy)) holiday aroma filled the warm kitchen.

3. Her fingernails on the chalkboard (hurt, (grated against)) my ears.

4. The condemned house emitted a (horrible, (putrid)) odor.

5. The antique coat was (old and torn, (worn and tattered)).

▶ **Write a short essay or a longer paragraph that creates an extraordinary sensory experience. Make sure you address at least three of the five senses by using the most effective words possible to evoke reader response. Use an additional piece of paper if needed.**

**Answers will vary**

_____

_____

_____

_____

WRITER'S CRAFT

# ▶ Making Inferences

The *theme* of a selection is its moral or meaning. The themes of fiction selections often focus on topics that are important to all people in some way. For example, love, friendship, family, and growing up are some popular theme topics. In order to determine a selection's theme, sometimes the reader must make inferences.

On the lines provided, state what you think the theme is for "Love As Strong As Ginger." Then write the clues from the story and the prior knowledge you used to infer the selection's moral or meaning.

**Inferred Theme:** _____

_____

**Text clues and Prior Knowledge about the Theme:**

_____

_____

_____

_____

_____

_____

_____

_____

_____

_____

# ▶ Consonant Blends

**Rhyming Strategy** Write two words that rhyme with each word below. The rhyming word must begin with a consonant blend.

| | | | |
|---|---|---|---|
| 1. | craze | graze | praise |
| 2. | threat | fret | sweat |
| 3. | thrown | blown | flown |
| 4. | sprint | glint | print |
| 5. | stripe | gripe | swipe |
| 6. | break | steak | flake |
| 7. | scrape | grape | drape |
| 8. | stray | gray | sway |
| 9. | strain | brain | drain |
| 10. | scheme | cream | steam |

Answers will vary. Sample answers shown.

**Pronunciation Strategy** Write two words not used above that begin with the consonant blend.

| | | | |
|---|---|---|---|
| 11. | scr | scramble | scribble |
| 12. | thr | throughout | thrash |
| 13. | spl | splash | split |
| 14. | str | string | strap |

Answers will vary. Sample answers shown.

SPELLING

**UNIT 3** Heritage • **Lesson 4** *Love As Strong As Ginger*

# ► Levels of Specificity

► The following series contain words that go from more specific to less specific or from less specific to more specific. Write a word on the line that fits the series.

Answers may vary.

1. mouth, _____teeth_____, incisor

2. _____Little Women_____, novel, book

3. North America, _____Florida_____, Miami

4. bumblebee, _____insect_____, animal

5. _____fir_____, conifer, tree

6. neighborhood, house, _____bedroom_____

7. peas, _____vegetable_____, food

8. school supply, writing utensil, _____pencil_____

9. calendar, _____month_____, August

10. body of water, _____lake_____, Lake Tahoe

11. _____chip_____, CPU, computer

► Replace the underlined words with words that are more specific. Write the new word(s) next to the underlined word. Answers will vary.

12. Thousands of years ago, <u>scientists</u> astronomers grouped stars together to form pictures called constellations.

13. I heard an <u>animal</u> jackal shriek wildly in the distance.

14. Dinosaurs lived <u>many</u> 225 to 65 million years ago.

15. I am going <u>overseas</u> for my summer vacation. to England

# ▶Conjunctions and Interjections

▶ Combine and rewrite these sentences using the following coordinating conjunctions: *and, but, or, so, yet, nor, for*. Use a different conjunction for each example. **Answers will vary.**

1. Josh sold tickets. Brandon ran the projector.

   _____

2. Carol caught the ball. Then she dropped it.

   _____

3. Come to class on time. Come to detention after school.

   _____

   _____

▶ Combine and rewrite these sentences using the following subordinating conjunctions: *after, although, before, if, when, while*. Use a different conjunction for each example.

   **Answers will vary.**

4. We got up early. The sun came over the hill.

   _____

5. Dad was washing the car. Jacob was mowing the lawn.

   _____

   _____

6. I can go to the movies with you. I must finish my social studies homework.

   _____

   _____

GRAMMAR AND USAGE

**UNIT 3** Heritage • **Lesson 4** *Love As Strong As Ginger*

# ▶ Sound of Language

1. Write a paragraph about an early memory. Use the title "I Remember When." Give your language sound by using *assonance* (the repeating of vowel sounds such as *rain, main, drain*) and *repetition* (the repeating of a word or phrase to add emphasis).

   **Students must use one example of *assonance* and one of**

   _____

   **repetition.**

   _____

   _____

   _____

2. Write a paragraph entitled "If I Were." Complete this sentence and use it in the beginning of your paragraph, "If I were a _____, I'd _____." Give your language sound by using *onomatopoeia* (this is a vocal imitation of a sound such as *buzz, thump,* and *snap*) and *alliteration* (repeating the beginning consonant sound such as *ship, shirt,* and *sharp*).

   **Students must use at least one example of *onomatopoeia***

   _____

   **and one example of *alliteration*.**

   _____

   _____

   _____

# ▶ Silent Letters

**Pronunciation Strategy** Write the word next to its pronunciation. All the words have silent letters.

1. /yot/    yacht

2. /nōm/    gnome

3. /rông/    wrong

4. /nash/    gnash

5. /rap′ sə dē/    rhapsody

6. /nol′ ij/    knowledge

7. /plum′ ər/    plumber

8. /sē′ nik/    scenic

9. /ī′ lənd/    island

10. /fas′ ən/    fasten

**SPELLING**

**Write the word that solves each word problem. Each word has a silent letter.**

11. wretched – tched + nch =    wrench

    What is the silent letter?    w

12. misery – ery + tletoe =    mistletoe

    What is the silent letter?    t

13. kingdom – k + g – dom + ham =    gingham

    What is the silent letter?    h

# ▶Antonyms

**VOCABULARY**

▶ The words in parentheses after each sentence are antonyms. Fill in each blank with the word that best completes the sentence.

1. The army was forced to _____retreat_____ after its defeat. (advance, retreat)

2. The United States _____exports_____ wheat and other grain products to countries that need them. (imports, exports)

3. The hurricane approaching from the south made the air very _____turbulent_____. (placid, turbulent)

4. As my eye scanned the page _____vertically_____, I noticed the words were bigger at the top than at the bottom. (vertically, horizontally)

5. When my model collapsed next to Jenny's, I realized mine was _____inferior_____. (superior, inferior)

▶ Write an antonym for the word in parentheses. Make sure it fits the sentence. Answers may vary.

6. I _____gathered_____ my papers before writing my final draft. (scattered)

7. It is important that the president have a _____positive_____ attitude about the future. (negative)

8. Although my vacation was _____brief_____, I enjoyed it tremendously. (lengthy)

9. The directions for assembling the computer were too _____complicated_____. (simple)

10. Her _____frugal_____ way of living enabled her to take a vacation once a year. (extravagant)

**UNIT 3** Heritage • **Lesson 5** *The Night Journey*

# ▶ Pronouns

▶ Underline the incorrect pronouns and write the correct forms above them.

1. Brenda and <u>her</u> went to the football game.
   *she*

2. The sergeant at the gate saluted Jimmy and <u>he</u>.
   *him*

3. Is <u>you're</u> desk too heavy to move?
   *your*

4. Marshall <u>hisself</u> has moved to Brooklyn with his brother.
   *himself*

5. It is <u>me</u> who has brought the pizza.
   *I*

▶ Write sentences using the following pronouns.

1. yourself: *Answers will vary.* _____

   _____

2. somebody: _____

   _____

3. their: _____

   _____

4. its: _____

   _____

5. several: _____

   _____

**GRAMMAR AND USAGE**

# Figurative Language

**WRITER'S CRAFT**

▶ Select three of the pairs below (or choose your own pairs) and write a sentence about each pair. One of the sentences should use a simile; one, a metaphor; and one, personification.

a kite and a hawk    a friend and a bridge         a dancer and a meadow
night and a person   a skyscraper and a mountain   electricity and a stream

1. Answers will vary. _____

   _____

2. _____

   _____

3. _____

   _____

▶ When using figurative language make sure you do not mix metaphors. Correct the following mixed metaphors. Possible answers are given.

1. In every shy person, there is a hidden tiger ready to take flight.

   In every shy person, there is a hidden tiger ready to

   spring out.

   _____

2. The clock's ticking reminded him of the beating of a drum that pounded against the shore of his brain.

   The clock's ticking reminded him of the beating of a

   drum.

   _____

# ▶Review

**Visualization Strategy** Write the word from each set that is spelled correctly.

1. <u>farther</u>

   oarbit

   impourtant

   farther

   arche

2. <u>bristle</u>

   brisle

   bristel

   bristle

   brissle

3. <u>allowed</u>

   crouded

   proul

   backgrownd

   allowed

4. <u>meddlesome</u>

   travle

   colossle

   cannible

   meddlesome

5. <u>apparel</u>

   crum

   apparel

   fowntain

   puple

6. <u>guard</u>

   physicle

   senery

   guard

   bizare

**SPELLING**

Name _____ Date _____

# ▶Review

**Use context clues to tell the meaning of the underlined words.**

1. Mrs. Jeffries told the class to stand in two <u>parallel</u> lines across from each other.

   **extending so as not to meet**

2. When Kathleen lost the race, she had a <u>sullen</u> look on her face.

   **gloomy**

3. The rain lasted only a <u>brief</u> time, and then we went outside for a walk.

   **short**

4. The <u>placid</u> sound of the waves hitting the shore was soothing to me.

   **calm**

5. We sailed past the high walls of the <u>canyon</u> on our rafting trip.

   **deep valley with steep sides, usually with a stream**

   **running through it.**

6. I bought a T-shirt in New York City as a <u>memento</u> of my trip.

   **a reminder of someone or something; keepsake; souvenir**

7. Nate spent a long time on the math problem because it <u>perplexed</u> him.

   **puzzled; troubled**

*Review* • Challenge

# ▶Review

▶Tell whether the underlined words are adjectives (Adj.) or adverbs (Adv.).

     Adj.           Adv. Adv.       Adj.Adj.
1. The <u>young</u> lawyer walked <u>very</u> <u>cautiously</u> into the <u>tall</u> <u>law</u> building.

     Adj.           Adv.      Adj.     Adv.
2. Our <u>space</u> probe landed <u>softly</u> on the <u>red</u> planet <u>yesterday</u>.

     Adj.    Adv. Adj.       Adv.       Adv.
3. That <u>tall</u> boy is <u>rather</u> <u>talented</u>; he'll go <u>far</u> if he works <u>hard</u>.

     Adj.        Adv.            Adj.    Adv.
4. The <u>dirty</u> plumbers <u>finally</u> finished cleaning the <u>old</u> pipes <u>today</u>.

▶Use these prepositional phrases in sentences. They may be used in any order. Answers will vary.

   **5.** on this street / during rush hour

_____

   **6.** about pirates / of the silvery moon

_____

▶Use this subordinating conjunction in a sentence. Answers will vary.

   **7.** when

_____

▶Use these pronouns and contractions in sentences. They may be used in any order. Answers will vary.

   **8.** your / you're

_____

   **9.** its / it's

_____

**GRAMMAR AND USAGE**

**WRITER'S CRAFT**

# ▶Exact Words

1. Rewrite the following paragraph replacing the underlined words with more precise, descriptive ones. You may add phrases and rearrange sentences as needed.

   We had a <u>fun</u> time at the zoo. We saw some <u>cool</u> animals and met some <u>nice</u> zookeepers who told us <u>stuff</u> about the animals. It was <u>neat</u> to <u>look at</u> some of the animals that we <u>saw</u> in our science books.

   _____

   _____

   _____

   _____

   _____

2. Practice using exact words by reviewing a selection from your writing folder. Replace words with more appropriate and accurate words wherever needed. Write the word and its replacement on the lines below.

   **Answers will vary.**

   _____

   _____

   _____

   _____

   _____

# ▶ Cause and Effect

## ▶ Multiple Causes and Effects

Some causes can bring about more than one effect. In turn, one effect might have several different causes. Look at these examples:

▶ **One cause with several effects:** *Because I didn't get much sleep last night, I was tired, I didn't feel well, and I did poorly on my history test.*

▶ **One effect with several causes:** *Mark could not hear his mother call him because his bedroom door was shut, he was on the telephone, and his stereo was blaring.*

**Practice writing relationships with multiple causes and effects in the space provided below.**

**One cause with several effects:**  Answers will vary.

_____

_____

_____

_____

**One effect with several causes:**

_____

_____

_____

_____

**COMPREHENSION**

Name _____  Date _____

SPELLING

# ▶ Plurals

**Conventions Strategy** Write the singular or plural form of one
of the words in the box to complete the sentences below.
Use each word once.

| pistachio | ratio | faculty | emergency | foe |
|---|---|---|---|---|
| waltz | postpone | flourish | naturalist | strategy |

1. The _____ratio_____ of rabbits to wolves in the
   forest is twelve to one.

2. Three different _____faculties_____ asked my father to
   come and teach at their universities.

3. As a special treat, my mom packed some _____pistachios_____
   in my lunch today.

4. The dancer added some special _____flourishes_____ to
   his dance to make it more dramatic.

5. Kobe wants to be a _____naturalist_____ at a national park.

6. My dad uses many different _____strategies_____ when
   he plays chess.

7. My parents love to dance _____waltzes_____ when
   they go ballroom dancing.

8. One _____foe_____ of a squirrel is a fox.

9. The fire department needs to be able to respond in case of
   _____emergencies_____.

Name _____ Date _____

# ►Social Studies Words

►Use one of the words in the box to complete each sentence. Use a dictionary if necessary.

| anarchy | tyranny | legislative | executive | judicial |
|---|---|---|---|---|

1. If there were no recognized government, the confusion and disorder that would result would be called
   **anarchy**
   _____ .

2. The **legislative** _____ branch of government is made up of Congress and is responsible for making laws.

3. When power is used in an unjust and cruel way, it is
   known as **tyranny** _____ .

4. The **judicial** _____ branch of government is responsible for the administration and interpretation of laws.

5. The **executive** _____ branch of government is responsible for enforcing the laws.

►Write a sentence using each word. Be sure to use the word in a social studies context.

   6. anarchy _____

   7. tyranny _____

   8. legislative _____

   9. executive _____

   10. judicial _____

**VOCABULARY**

# Types of Sentences

**Rewrite this paragraph correcting all fragments and run-on sentences.**

Before we went to school. We had to wait for the bus it was very late. When we arrived at school we were all tardy but it was excused. My teacher already. Started the lesson. My friend helped me catch up she told me what page we were on and I caught up very quickly but then we had to go to lunch and I had forgotten my money.  The day didn't go well. Tomorrow.

Answers will vary. Possible answer shown.

We ate breakfast before we went to school. We had to

wait for the bus, and it was very late. When we arrived at

school, we were all tardy; but it was excused. My teacher

already knew we were going to be late, so she started the

lesson. My friend helped me catch up. She told me what

page we were on. I caught up very quickly. Then we had to

go to lunch, but I had forgotten my money. The day didn't

go well. Oh well, there's always tomorrow.

_____

_____

_____

_____

GRAMMAR AND USAGE

# ▶ Aim/Purpose/Audience

**Using the information given below, write a one to three sentence opening or introduction. Adjust what you say to the needs and interests of your audience. To do this, you must keep in mind what your audience knows already, what attitudes your audience has toward a subject, and what interest the audience has in the subject.**

| Writer | Document and Purpose |
|---|---|
| Dog owner | Write a letter to the city council to request enforcement of the leash laws in the local parks. |

_____

_____

_____

_____

| Coach | Write a letter asking the school board for new uniforms. |
|---|---|

_____

_____

_____

_____

| Fifth grader | Write a paragraph to your cousin explaining how to do something. |
|---|---|

_____

_____

_____

_____

**WRITER'S CRAFT**

**SPELLING**

# ▶ Possessive Nouns

**Conventions Strategy** Complete the sentence using the correct singular possessive form of the underlined word.

1.  lawyer:    The __lawyer's__ briefcase was sitting on the desk.

2.  heiress:   The __heiress's__ fortune gave her the luxury of traveling around the world.

3.  referee:   The __referee's__ whistle is blown to signal the start of the game.

4.  lady:      The __lady's__ purse was black with a brown shoulder strap.

5.  monkey:    The __monkey's__ cage was kept very clean.

**Complete the sentence using the correct plural possessive form of the underlined word.**

6.  lawyer:    The __lawyers'__ briefcases were sitting on the desk.

7.  heiress:   The __heiresses'__ fortunes enabled them to travel around the world.

8.  referee:   The __referees'__ whistles are blown to signal the start of the game.

9.  lady:      The __ladies'__ purses were black with brown shoulder straps.

10. monkey:    The __monkeys'__ cages were kept very clean.

*Possessive Nouns* • Challenge

# ▶Synonyms

**Write two synonyms for the underlined word.**

Answers will vary. Possible answers shown.

1. Patrick had an <u>uncanny</u> ability to always guess what I was thinking.

   eerie, weird

   creepy, spooky

2. I didn't mean to <u>provoke</u> an argument when I said the Bearcats were my favorite team.

   incite, instigate

   inflame, foment

3. Lawanda was <u>shrewd</u> when it came to making business decisions.

   cunning, insightful

   wily, astute

4. It really <u>irks</u> me when people in the library are making too much noise.

   annoys

   irritates

5. The teacher said <u>emphatically</u>, "Stop talking!"

   strongly

   boldly

6. The teacher was <u>outraged</u> when the students didn't listen.

   insulted

   offended

**VOCABULARY**

# Subject and Verb Agreement

GRAMMAR AND USAGE

▶ Edit these examples for subject verb agreement. Write the correct verb above the incorrect verb.

        **is**
She are extremely happy to see her cousins at

               **arrive**
family reunions. We often arrives early to have more

time to talk.

                           **talks**
Valerie, who is Melissa's friend, still talk about her

             **remembers**
first airplane ride. She remember that she asked the

person sitting next to her how to use the telephone.

                           **was**
She actually called her home while she were flying.

▶ Change this present tense paragraph to past tense. Write the correct verb forms above the incorrect verb forms.

    **were**                       **was**
We are on our way to California. Mom is sitting in

the front seat next to Dad. After traveling for an hour,
  **stopped**                    **fixed**
we stop at a road side rest for lunch. Mom fixes the
           **poured**
sandwiches while Dad pours the drinks. My little
   **ran**   **skinned**         **put**
brother runs off and skins his knee. Dad puts a
                  **jumped**
bandage on his wound, and we all jump back into the
      **fell**               **arrived**
car. After a while, I fall asleep. Upon waking we arrive
     **swam**  **ate**       **went**
at the motel. We swim and eat dinner and go to bed.
   **giggled**     **yelled**
My brother and I giggle until my dad yells at us. Then
 **went**
we go to sleep.

Name _____ Date _____

# Transition Words

Transition words show how details are related, and they make writing easier to follow. Without these words, you just have a list of details.

1. Insert connecting words to help this paragraph read more smoothly.

   Doctors warn that people are eating too much salt in their daily diets. These experts have estimated that the consumption of five grams of salt per day is all right for most people. Doctors claim that many people consume between ten and twenty-four grams of salt daily. They advise patients to restrict or even eliminate the use of salt in cooking or at the table. Doctors encourage patients to avoid some processed foods that contain salt as an additive.

   Possible answers are *For example,* at beginning of sentence two; *Therefore,* at beginning of sentence four; *Also,* at beginning of sentence five.

2. Read the list of topics and write the type of connecting words you might use to help the sentences flow smoothly.

| Paragraph Topic | Connecting-Word Type |
|---|---|
| Winning the Championship | Possible answer might include chronological order words. |
| The Beautiful Coast | Possible answer might be place or location words |
| Making Pizza | Possible answer might include chronological order words |
| Reducing Sports Injuries | Possible answer might include order of importance words |

**WRITER'S CRAFT**

# ▶ Compound Words

**SPELLING**

**Meaning Strategy** Use a compound word to complete the sentence.

1. I can go swimming with my watch on since it's __waterproof__.

2. If you are an honest, dependable, reliable person who can be counted on, then you are someone who is __trustworthy__.

3. If you go to Niagara you can see one of the world's largest __waterfalls__.

4. You might go to a pharmacy or a __drugstore__ to get a prescription filled.

5. I had to use the __drawbridge__ to cross the moat and get into the castle.

6. To __download__ is to transfer information from a larger computer to a smaller one.

7. When you take your pulse, you are measuring your __heartbeat__.

8. When I was swimming in the ocean, I got stung by the tentacles of a __jellyfish__.

9. A puzzle with words that you fill across and down is a __crossword__.

10. We built a __sandcastle__ on the beach.

*Compound Words* • **Challenge**

# ▶Figurative Language

▶Write on the line whether a simile, metaphor, or the use of personification is underlined in the sentences. Explain the meaning of the simile, metaphor, or personification on the second line.

As the wind blew, the <u>flowers danced</u> about in the garden.

1. personification

2. the flowers moved, giving the impression that they were dancing

After she hit the ball, <u>Mycha ran like the wind</u> to first base.

3. simile

4. ran very fast

<u>Sasha is a butterfly</u> when she daintily floats through her ballet performance.

5. metaphor

6. dances lightly and delicately

▶Write a sentence of your own using personification.

7. _____ Answers will vary. _____

▶Write a sentence of your own using a simile.

8. _____ Answers will vary. _____

▶Write a sentence of your own using a metaphor.

9. _____

VOCABULARY

# ►Misused Words

**Write sentences using the following instructions.**

**Answers will vary.**

**1.** Use *lie* in a sentence about the beach.

_____

**2.** Use *lay* (as in placing) in a sentence about the beach.

_____

**3.** Use *laid* in a sentence about dishes.

_____

**4.** Use *lain* in a sentence about a cat.

_____

**5.** Use *sit* in a sentence about a concert.

_____

**6.** Use *set* in a sentence about plants.

_____

**7.** Use *it's* in a sentence about a mouse.

_____

**8.** Use *its* in a sentence about a whale.

_____

GRAMMAR AND USAGE

# ▶ Sentence Elaboration and Expansion

**WRITER'S CRAFT**

1. Combine these sentences and put them into a paragraph.

England is in the British Isles. Scotland is in the British Isles.
My Aunt Jan visited England. Aunt Jan visited Scotland.
She climbed mountains in Scotland. She visited gardens in England.
Jan sipped tea in the afternoon. Jan ate scones in the afternoon.

**Possible paragraphs may read like:** *My Aunt Jan went to*

*the British Isles last summer and visited England and*

*Scotland. She showed us pictures of her visiting gardens*

*in England and climbing mountains in Scotland.*

*According to Aunt Jan, the most relaxing part of her trip*

*was when she had tea and scones each afternoon.*

2. Combine at least two of these sentences by using appositives.

New York City has more than seven and a half million
people. It is one of the largest cities in the world. New York
is an important center for business, culture, and trade. It is
also the home of the United Nations. The city has banks,
stock exchanges, and other financial institutions. These
institutions are located in the famous Wall Street area of
the city.

**Possible answers may include:** *New York City, one of the*

*largest cities in the world, has more than seven and a half*

*million people. New York, an important center for business,*

*culture and trade, is also home of the United Nations.*

**UNIT 4** Making a New Nation • **Lesson 4** *The Declaration of Independence*

# ►Classifying and Categorizing

From your experience, you have probably learned that it is easier to classify things than it is to classify ideas. Because ideas are abstract and can be interpreted in different ways, it is sometimes difficult to assign them to specific categories. In the space below, create a chart of some of your ideas about the theme Making a New Nation. You might use headings such as *Prior Knowledge* and *What I Want to Learn* or *Ideas About the Colonies* and *Ideas About England*. Your category headings will depend on the ideas you list.

# ▶Changing *y* to *i*

**Conventions Strategy** Complete the sentences using one of the words in the box. You may need to add *-er*, *-ed*, *-es*, or *-ing* to the ending of the word.

| tragedy | friendly | survey | supply | hurry |
|---------|----------|--------|--------|-------|
| pastry | petrify | classify | preoccupy | deny |

1. I __surveyed__ all of the students in my class for a paper I was writing.

2. Carrie was __preoccupied__ with her homework when the telephone rang.

3. Sometimes organic matter __petrifies__ into a stony material over many, many years.

4. Shakespeare wrote comedies and __tragedies__.

5. Michael is __friendlier__ than Sally.

6. We purchased all of the necessary __supplies__ before we started to paint the house.

7. The __pastries__ we ate at the bakery were delicious.

8. The information was __classified__, so it was not available to the general public.

9. We __hurried__ to the bus stop so that we wouldn't miss the bus.

10. Sarah __denied__ that she had taken cookies from the jar.

SPELLING

# Base Word Families

**VOCABULARY**

**For each word, write the base word and one more word in the word family.**

**Answers will vary. Possibilities shown.**

**1.** specialize

Base word: __special__

Family word: __specialist, specially__

**2.** revising

Base word: __revise__

Family word: __revision__

**3.** responsive

Base word: __response__

Family word: __responsively, respond__

**4.** resentful

Base word: __resent__

Family word: __resentment__

**5.** undecided

Base word: __decide__

Family word: __decision__

**6.** energetic

Base word: __energy__

Family word: __energetically__

Name _____ Date _____

**UNIT 4** Making a New Nation • **Lesson 4** *The Declaration of Independence*

# ▶Comparative and Superlative Adjectives and Adverbs

**Interview a friend. Write sentences using the following guidelines comparing and contrasting your likenesses and differences. Use comparative and superlative adjectives and adverbs in all of your sentences.**

1. Compare your height.          **Answers will vary.**

_____

_____

2. Compare your two heights with one other person.

_____

_____

3. Compare your hair color.

_____

_____

4. Compare your running speed.

_____

_____

5. Compare your running speed with everyone else in the class.

_____

_____

**GRAMMAR AND USAGE**

# ▶Passive Voice

1. Look at several of your recent writing selections or pieces of writing by others that you particularly like. Find five examples each of the active voice and passive voice. Convert each of the examples to the other voice. Comment about the difference in emphasis and rhythm change.

_____

_____

_____

_____

_____

_____

_____

_____

_____

_____

_____

_____

_____

_____

_____

_____

_____

# ▶Drawing Conclusions

When investigating a topic, researchers use multiple sources to answer questions they have raised about the topic. Think of a question you have that relates to the theme "Making a New Nation." This question may stem from the selection "The Master Spy of Yorktown" or from other reading you have done on the unit theme. Use information from two or more sources to draw a conclusion that answers your question. Then, in the space below, write a paragraph using your conclusion as the topic sentence. Provide at least three clues from the sources you used to support your conclusion.

_____

_____

_____

_____

_____

_____

_____

_____

_____

_____

_____

_____

**COMPREHENSION**

# ▶ Doubling Final Consonants

**Conventions Strategy** Write the base word for the following words that end in *-ed* or *-ing*.

1. hopping  hop
2. hoping  hope
3. wagged  wag
4. waged  wage

5. scraped  scrape
6. scrapped  scrap
7. taped  tape
8. tapped  tap

**Complete the sentences using one of the words in the box. You will need to add *-ed* or *-ing*.**

| plow | delay | jump | flop | poll | sit | clog |
|------|-------|------|------|------|-----|------|

9. Our flight was **delayed** three hours due to bad weather.

10. I **polled** the students in our class to see who they wanted for president.

11. The movie **flopped** despite the good reviews by the critics.

12. I spent all day Saturday **plowing** the fields.

13. Shannon was **jumping** rope with Alison.

14. The drain was **clogged** and the sink was filling up with water.

15. I was **sitting** at my desk when the fire alarm rang.

*Doubling Final Consonants* • Challenge

SPELLING

**UNIT 4** Making a New Nation • **Lesson 5** *The Master Spy of Yorktown*

# ▶ Words with Multiple Meanings

**The underlined words in the sentences are verbs. They also can be used as nouns with different meanings. Write a sentence using the word as a noun with a different meaning. Then, write the meaning of the word on the line.**
Answers will vary. Possible sentences and meanings shown.
**1.** Sheldon didn't <u>break</u> his leg when he went skiing.

We'll take a break after we're done with this lesson.
_____

meaning: a rest or a stop _____

**2.** I didn't want to <u>peer</u> too closely into the microscope.

Rosa is in the same class and is a peer. _____

_____

meaning: a person of the same rank, value; an equal _____

**3.** I <u>will</u> go to the zoo on Sunday.

They read his will after the funeral. _____

_____

meaning: a legal document containing one's final wishes ____

**4.** Marshall will <u>address</u> the audience after the dinner.

Abraham Lincoln wrote the *Gettysburg Address*. _____

_____

meaning: a written or spoken speech _____

**VOCABULARY**

**UNIT 4** Making a New Nation • **Lesson 5** *The Master Spy of Yorktown*

# ► Direct and Indirect Objects

**GRAMMAR AND USAGE**

► **Fill in the blanks with direct objects and indirect objects.**

**Answers will vary.**

1. Thomas gave his _____ a _____.

2. Every year, Sammy sends _____ _____.

3. My dad bought our _____ a new _____.

4. Doctor Brown showed her _____ another _____.

5. Michael sent _____ and _____ a _____.

► **Follow the directions when writing these sentences.**

**Answers will vary.**

1. Write a sentence with a direct object.

_____

2. Write a sentence with an indirect object.

_____

3. Write a sentence with a compound direct object.

_____

4. Write a sentence with a compound indirect object.

_____

5. Write a sentence with a compound indirect object and
a compound direct object.

_____

# ▶Developing Persuasive Writing

**Answer the questions and follow the directions to help you develop a persuasive essay.** Answers will vary.

**1.** Choose a topic for your essay.

_____

_____

**2.** What evidence do you have to prove your point?

_____

_____

**3.** What arguments will be given against yours?

_____

_____

**4.** How can you answer these arguments?

_____

_____

**5.** Can you support your points with evidence? How?

_____

_____

**WRITER'S CRAFT**

**UNIT 4** Making a New Nation • **Lesson 6** *Shh! We're Writing the Constitution*

# ▶ Fact and Opinion

COMPREHENSION

When authors write to persuade, they are very likely to include opinions and try to get their readers to agree with their opinions. One key to good persuasive writing is that the opinions are supported by facts. Choose a topic related to "Making a New Nation" about which you have a strong opinion. Then, write a paragraph about that topic. Remember that your goal is to persuade readers to agree with your opinion. Be sure to support your opinion with facts.

_____

_____

_____

_____

_____

_____

_____

_____

_____

_____

_____

_____

_____

_____

*Fact and Opinion* • **Challenge**

**UNIT 4** Making a New Nation • **Lesson 6** *Shh! We're Writing the Constitution*

# ▶Dropping *e* and Adding Endings

**Conventions Strategy** Complete the sentences using one of the words in the box. You will need to add *-ed, y,* or *-ing*.

| flake | shade | confide | stimulate | sneeze |
|-------|-------|---------|-----------|--------|
| slice | place | issue | amaze | expire |

**SPELLING**

1. It was very __shady__ underneath the trees.

2. Tasha __confided__ in me because she knew I was a trustworthy friend.

3. I could not use the coupon because it had __expired__.

4. Because of my allergies, I cannot stop __sneezing__ when I am around cats.

5. The dinnertime conversation at my house is often very __stimulating__.

6. I was __amazed__ to learn that Mozart wrote his first symphony when he was five.

7. I'll be __slicing__ my birthday cake after I blow out the candles.

8. The school will be __issuing__ textbooks on the first day of school.

9. The pastry was so __flaky__ it crumbled in my hands.

10. She __placed__ her fingers on the keys and began to play the piano.

**UNIT 4**  Making a New Nation • **Lesson 6** *Shh! We're Writing the Constitution*

# ►Word Origins

**VOCABULARY**

►*Aster* or *astr* is a Greek root. Write three words that use this root.  **Answers will vary.**

1. astronomy _____

2. asteroid _____

3. astrology, astronaut _____

What do you think the root *aster* or *astr* means? star _____

►*Cycl* is a Greek root. Write three words that use this root.

4. bicycle  **Answers will vary.** _____

5. cyclone _____

6. cyclical _____

What do you think the root *cycl* means? circle _____

►*Rupt* is a Latin root. Write three words that use this root.

7. disrupt  **Answers will vary.** _____

8. interruption _____

9. rupture _____

What do you think the root *rupt* means? to break _____

►*Sens* is a Latin root. Write three words that use this root.

10. sensitive  **Answers will vary.** _____

11. sensible _____

12. insensitive _____

What do you think the root *sens* means? to feel _____

# ▶ Contractions, Negatives, and Double Negatives

**This is a formal paragraph. Edit out all contractions and double negatives.**

Each year all students participate in the school

science fair. This year there ~~aren't~~ *are not* any new rules. After

school on Tuesday, February 6, students ~~shouldn't~~ *should not* stay

after school but go home to collect their projects. No

one will be allowed to set up ~~no~~ *any* projects until 4:30.

Until that time there ~~won't~~ *will not* be ~~no~~ *any* electricity available.

Students should put their projects in the assigned

locations and wait to be judged. Nobody will be

allowed in the area except participants. The judges

~~can't~~ *cannot* answer ~~no~~ *any* questions until after all projects are

judged. At that time, everyone should assemble in the

gym for awards.

# ▶Outlining

**Organize and use the items provided in the list below to complete the following outline. Keep in mind the subject statement as you organize.**

Subject statement: People who live in apartments should be allowed to keep dogs.

| | | |
|---|---|---|
| Dogs can be good tenants | Emotional Health | Owner's responsibilities |
| | Landlord's responsibilities | Social Skills |
| Dogs provide security | Companionship | Barking |
| Physical Health | Responsibility | Dogs contribute to good health |

I. Dogs Contribute to Good Health

   A. Physical Health

   B. Emotional Health

      1. Companionship

      2. Responsibility

      3. Social Skills

II. Dogs Provide Security

   A. Barking

III. Dogs Can Be Good Tenants

   A. Owner's Responsibilities

   B. Landlord's Responsibilities

# ▶ Parallelism

**Practice using parallel forms. Change the *italicized* elements to make the items parallel.**

1. The warm-up includes *stretches*, *sit-ups*, and *sprinting*.

   Possible answer may be: The warm-up includes *stretches, sit-ups, and sprints.*

   _____

2. The group had tried *pleading*, *threats*, and *shouting*.

   Possible answer: The group had tried *pleading, threatening, and shouting.*

   _____

3. The kitchen crew *scraped the grill*, *the shakers were refilled*, and *were taking out the trash*.

   The kitchen crew *scraped the grill, refilled the salt shakers, and took out the trash.*

   _____

4. The job required *baby-sitting*, *house-cleaning*, and *the preparation of the meals*.

   The job required *baby-sitting, house-cleaning and preparing the meals.*

   _____

WRITER'S CRAFT

**COMPREHENSION**

# ▶ Main Idea and Details

As you learned earlier in this lesson main ideas are sometimes directly stated and other times they are implied. Write a paragraph about a topic of your choice in the space below. Do not state the main idea directly. Instead, imply it by using strong supporting details. Then, exchange paragraphs with a classmate and try to determine the main idea of each other's paragraph.

_____

_____

_____

_____

_____

_____

_____

_____

_____

_____

_____

_____

_____

_____

_____

# ▶Review

**Conventions Strategy** Complete the sentences using one of the words in the box. You will need to add an ending to the word to make it fit the sentence.

| confuse | pry | indulge | imitate | plug | satisfy | plod |
|---------|-----|---------|---------|------|---------|------|

1. I thought the math homework was <u>confusing</u> until my brother helped me with it.

2. We were <u>plodding</u> along the trail at a slow, steady pace.

3. If the computer is not <u>plugged</u> in, then it won't work.

4. The winners were <u>satisfied</u> with the election results.

5. The impressionist <u>imitated</u> the famous actor.

6. My parents <u>indulged</u> my love of soccer by sending me to soccer camp.

7. My diary is not open to <u>prying</u> eyes.

**SPELLING**

**UNIT 4**  Making a New Nation • **Lesson 7** *We, the People of the United States*

# ▶Review

**VOCABULARY**

▶ Use one of the words in the box to complete the sentences. Use a dictionary if necessary.

| federal | rebellion | revolution | parties | Congress |
|---------|-----------|------------|---------|----------|

1. The __Congress__ of the United States is made up of the Senate and the House of Representatives.

2. A __revolution__ is an overthrow of an existing government.

3. An organized, unsuccessful attempt to overthrow a government is known as a __rebellion__.

4. Political __parties__ are established to promote particular theories of government.

▶ Write a sentence using each word. Be sure to use the word in a social studies context.

5. Congress _____

_____

6. revolution _____

_____

7. rebellion _____

_____

8. parties _____

_____

Name _____ Date _____

# Review

▶ **Make these dependent clauses sentences by adding an independent clause.**    **Answers will vary.**

1. Although he liked going to college.

   _____

2. Before Manny could get his driver's license.

   _____

▶ **Edit these sentences for verb forms, comparative and superlative forms, and misused words.**

         written         best

3. Tami has ~~wrote~~ a note to her ~~better~~ friend in the whole class.

   May  sit

4. ~~Can~~ I ~~set~~ in the seat near the window?

       lain                 worse

5. Linda has ~~laid~~ in the sun again and has a ~~worst~~ burn than yesterday.

▶ **Write the following sentences.**

6. Write a sentence about a birthday using a direct object and an indirect object.

   _____

7. Write a sentence about fall using a contraction.

   _____

**GRAMMAR AND USAGE**

**WRITER'S CRAFT**

# ▶ Sentence Variety

Does your writing seem boring? Let your writing reflect your personality and style by using sentence variety. To add interest to your writing, try varying the length of your sentences, the structure, and the openings.

1. Examine a piece of your own writing. First, count the number of sentences in each paragraph, noting those with the most and least number of sentences. Next, look for any variation and explain the effectiveness of the variation.

   **Answers vary. Students may comment that the variation**

   **makes writing more interesting and it changes the rhythm**

   **and flow of the writing.**

2. Examine that same selection for the number of words in sentences. Count the number of words in each sentence noting the sentences with the most and the least words. Can you explain any variations? Is the variation effective?

   **Answers will vary. The findings should help them become**

   **aware of the pace and rhythm of their writing.**

**UNIT 4** Making a New Nation • **Lesson 7** *We, the People of the United States*

# ▶Organizing Persuasive Writing

Prepare to write a persuasive essay by laying out your main ideas and details in the graphic organizer shown below. Remember that you will need to support your opinion using effective facts and information. First, choose a subject or focus of personal interest—something about which you feel strongly.

**WRITER'S CRAFT**

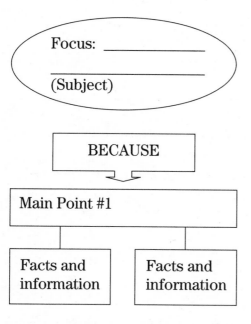

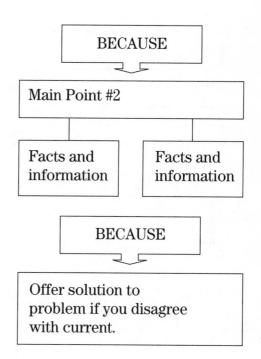

**Students should focus on a subject that is current and somewhat controversial. The facts and information are the ideas supporting their reasons. Make sure students become aware of opinions different from their own. They will need to address these issues in their writing.**

# ▶ Drawing Conclusions

**COMPREHENSION**

Lewis and Clark and their expedition met with many hardships on their journey west. Using evidence found in "Sacagawea's Journey," draw a conclusion about why the group persevered in the face of so much hardship. In the space below, write a paragraph using your conclusion as the topic sentence. Provide at least three clues from the text to support your conclusion. **Answers will vary.**

_____

_____

_____

_____

_____

_____

_____

_____

_____

_____

_____

_____

_____

_____

# Homophones

**Meaning Strategy**

In each sentence a word is underlined. Write a homophone for that word on the line. Then write a sentence using the homophone.

Cindy and Katrina <u>rowed</u> the boat across the lake.

1. road _____      _____
   Answers will vary. _____

Magazines are also called <u>serial</u> publications.

2. cereal _____      _____
   Answers will vary. _____

"Please shut the <u>gate</u> after you come into the yard," said Mrs. Alvarez.

3. gait _____      _____
   Answers will vary. _____

I just finished reading the <u>foreword</u> and I can't wait to start the book.

4. forward _____      _____
   Answers will vary. _____

John <u>mustered</u> enough strength to move the rock out of the way.

5. mustard _____      _____
   Answers will vary. _____

**SPELLING**

# ►Concept Words

►**Read the following paragraph. Concept words are underlined.**

Explorers are sent on <u>expeditions</u> to evaluate and investigate new lands. They often don't know how long their journeys will last, so they need to bring <u>provisions</u> that will last for a long time. A <u>cartographer</u> may accompany the explorers to chart their journey; they have to be prepared to confront many different types of <u>geological</u> features. Sometimes the explorers send out a <u>reconnaissance</u> mission to report back on what lies ahead for the main expedition. They often don't know whether or not they will encounter an <u>indigenous</u> population.

►**Write definitions for the underlined words.**

1. expeditions: a journey or excursion made for a
   specific purpose

2. provisions: something that is given or supplied; stock

3. cartographer: a mapmaker

4. geological: of or relating to the composition or structure
   of the earth

5. reconnaissance: an examination or survey to obtain
   information

6. indigenous: originating in a particular place

**VOCABULARY**

# Fragments

**Turn these fragments into sentences, and arrange them into a paragraph. Include additional information as needed.**

**Answers will vary.**

1. gathering wood to make a fire

2. after cooking the meal

3. just before dark

4. went on a camping trip to Mohican State Park

5. the two-man tent with mosquito netting

6. leaving the car in the parking lot, they

7. took a hike

8. will certainly do this again

9. the sleeping bags

_____

_____

_____

_____

_____

_____

_____

_____

# ▶ Main Idea and Details

**COMPREHENSION**

Following are six sentences that, when arranged correctly, create *two* paragraphs about the Plains Indians and buffalo. There is a topic sentence that states the main idea for each paragraph. The first paragraph includes information about why buffalo were important to the Plains Indians. The second paragraph explains what happened after the buffalo herds dwindled. First, number the sentences in the correct order. Then, on a separate piece of paper, write the paragraphs with the sentences in the correct order.

Answers will vary. Possible answers are shown.

4____ The way of life of the Plains Indians changed dramatically when the buffalo were gone.

1____ The Plains Indians depended on buffalo to provide much of what they needed to stay alive.

6____ Many had to move to reservations in order to avoid disease and starvation.

2____ The buffalo were a source of food for entire communities and provided building materials for shelters.

3____ Parts of the buffalo were used to make clothing, weapons, tools, and toys for their children.

5____ They were no longer able to provide for their own basic needs, and they found it difficult to survive and protect themselves.

**UNIT 5** Going West • **Lesson 2** *Buffalo Hunt*

# ▶Words with *dis-* and *mis-*

**SPELLING**

## Meaning Strategy
Complete the sentences using the words in the box. You will need
to add either *dis-* or *mis-* to the words. Use each word once.

| | | | | |
|---|---|---|---|---|
| tribute | guise | fortune | pleasure | courage |
| leading | represent | calculated | quote | qualified |

1. It is illegal to give __misleading__ testimony as a witness in the
   court of law.

2. I didn't recognize Dwayne when he came to my house wearing a
   __disguise__.

3. Mr. Tin asked me to __distribute__ the worksheets to the class.

4. The reporter wrote down the exact words of the interviewee so the
   newspaper article would not __misquote__ him.

5. The swimmer's false start caused him to be __disqualified__.

6. Shauna had the __misfortune__ of running out of gas while
   driving to work.

7. Mrs. Bing would certainly not __discourage__ us from studying
   for the math exam.

8. When candidates are running for president, they should not
   __misrepresent__ their views.

9. My mom expressed her __displeasure__ with my messy room.

10. I had __miscalculated__ the answer to the math problem.

Name _____ Date _____

# ▶Synonyms

**VOCABULARY**

Use context clues to choose the most appropriate synonym for the underlined word in each sentence. Then write a new sentence using the synonym.   **Answers will vary. Possible answers shown.**

1. When moving to a new house, we used trucks to <u>move</u> our belongings.

   **transport** _____

   **Answers will vary.** _____

2. The police were trying to determine a <u>reason</u> for the crime.

   **motive** _____

   **Answers will vary.** _____

3. After playing for 35 minutes, the basketball team became <u>tired</u>.

   **fatigued** _____

   **Answers will vary.** _____

4. The president <u>assigns</u> responsibility to members of his staff.

   **delegates** _____

   **Answers will vary.** _____

5. Napoleon was <u>ejected</u> from France after his reign.

   **exiled** _____

   **Answers will vary.** _____

6. I asked my teacher to <u>suggest</u> a few books that I should read.

   **recommend** _____

   **Answers will vary.** _____

# ▶Commas With Introductory Phrases

**1.** Write two sentences with long introductory phrases.

**Answers will vary.**

_____

_____

_____

_____

**2.** Write two sentences with short introductory phrases.

_____

_____

_____

_____

**3.** Write two sentences with introductory clauses.

_____

_____

_____

_____

Trade with a partner to see if your sentences are correct.

**MECHANICS**

**COMPREHENSION**

# ▶Sequence

Sequence plays an important role in stories, but it plays an even more important role in instructions. Imagine if you were trying to put together a bicycle and all of the instructions were out of order. It would be a nearly impossible task. Think about something you know how to do well, such as a game or a craft. Then write instructions on how to do it. Be sure you include each step in its proper sequence and include time words and order words such as *first, next, then,* and *finally.*

_____

_____

_____

_____

_____

_____

_____

_____

_____

_____

_____

_____

_____

_____

*Sequence* • Challenge

**UNIT 5** Going West • **Lesson 3** *The Journal of Wong Ming-Chung*

# ▶ Words with *-ent* and *-ant*

**Pronunciation Strategy**
Write the word for each respelling below.

1. /kən vûr′ sənt/    **conversant**

2. /ek spek′ tənt/    **expectant**

3. /i kwiv′ ə lənt/    **equivalent**

4. /ə mend′ mənt/    **amendment**

5. /kom′ plə mənt/    **compliment**

**Proofread the following story. Cross out each misspelled word and write the word correctly above it.**

                          **decent**    **prominent**
Professor Bolt, a ~~deccent~~ and ~~promenant~~ man,

stepped into a telephone booth and turned into a dog.
                             **present**
Can it be true? One witness was ~~presant~~ at the scene.
              **resident**
The witness, a local ~~resedent~~ named Mrs. Pringle, was
       **comment**             **evident**
asked to ~~commant~~. She said it was ~~evidant~~ that
                            **confident**
Professor Bolt turned into a dog. She is ~~confidant~~, and

her eyesight is perfect.
                 **recent**
"It looks like his ~~resent~~ invention for turning

people into dogs is a success," said Mrs. Pringle. "I
         **permanent**
hope it's not ~~permanint~~ !"

# Words with Multiple Meanings

**VOCABULARY**

Definitions are given for the words in the box. Write each word next to the correct definition. Use each word twice.

| course | difference | fortune | mean | stem | seal |
|--------|-----------|---------|------|------|------|

1. stem _____ to stop the flow or restrain

2. mean _____ a mathematical average

3. seal _____ to fasten or shut firmly, make watertight

4. mean _____ to intend to do something

5. course _____ a class or one unit of study

6. fortune _____ something that is going to happen to a person

7. stem _____ the main axis of a plant which supports leaves or flowers

8. seal _____ something that serves to authenticate, secure, or confirm

9. course _____ moving from one point to the next

10. difference _____ state or quality of being unlike

11. difference _____ the remainder left after subtracting one quantity from another

12. fortune _____ great wealth, a large sum of money

# ▶ Punctuation and Capitalization in Friendly Letters

**Write a friendly letter to your fourth grade teacher about something you liked in his/her class last year. Be sure to include the heading, greeting, body, closing, and signature.**
Answers will vary.

_____

_____

_____

_____

_____

_____

_____

_____

_____

_____

_____

_____

_____

_____

_____

_____

**MECHANICS**

**UNIT 5** **Going West • Lesson 3** *The Journal of Wong Ming-Chung*

**WRITER'S CRAFT**

# ▶ Structure of a Personal Letter

The structure of a personal letter includes the *heading*,
*salutation*, *body*, *closing*, and *signature*.

**Identify a wish or dream you have. Express your idea in at least a
three paragraph letter to your best friend. Include the elements for
the proper structure of a personal letter. Follow the correct
format, spacing, margins, indentations, and punctuation.**
Answers will vary. Students should include address in upper

right; date is in upper right; greeting is followed by a

comma; paragraphs are indented and separated by spaces;

closing has the first word capitalized and is followed by a

comma.

_____

_____

_____

_____

_____

_____

_____

_____

**UNIT 5** Going West • **Lesson 4** *The Coming of the Long Knives*

# ▶ Words with -tion, -sion, or -sure

## Pronunciation Strategy
Write the word for each respelling below.

1. /mish′ ən/  **mission**

2. /kon′ vûr sā′ shən/  **conversation**

3. /ek spō′ zhər/  **exposure**

4. /ek′ splə nā′ shən/  **explanation**

5. /presh′ ər/  **pressure**

**Complete the sentences with a word that ends in *-tion, -sion*, or *-sure*.**  Answers may vary.

6. Many scuba divers would love to come across a sunken **treasure**.

7. "Did you receive your **invitation** to my birthday party?" asked Denise.

8. If you have 20-20 **vision**, then you don't need glasses or contacts.

9. I really like the color **illustrations** in this book.

10. Time that you are free to spend doing whatever you want is known as **leisure** time.

SPELLING

**UNIT 5** Going West • **Lesson 4** *The Coming of the Long Knives*

# ◢ Foreign Words

**VOCABULARY**

▶ **Write a definition for the following French words and use them in a sentence.**

1. gourmet: <u>a person who likes and is an excellent judge of</u>
   <u>fine foods</u>

   <u>Answers will vary.</u>

2. croissant: <u>a roll in the shape of a crescent</u>

   <u>Answers will vary.</u>

▶ **Write a definition for the following Italian words and use them in a sentence.**

3. carnival: <u>an amusement show, usually one that travels</u>

   <u>Answers will vary.</u>

4. graffiti: <u>drawings or writings on walls, sidewalks or other</u>
   <u>surfaces</u>

   <u>Answers will vary.</u>

▶ **Write a definition for the following Japanese words and use them in a sentence.**

5. bonsai: <u>the art of growing miniature plants</u>

   <u>Answers will vary.</u>

6. haiku: <u>Japanese verse form in three lines containing</u>
   <u>seventeen syllables</u>

   <u>Answers will vary.</u>

Name _____ Date _____

# ▶ Punctuation and Capitalization in Business Letters

**Write a business letter to a local zoo or museum requesting information about volunteer activities. Be sure to include a heading, an inside address, a greeting, a body, a closing, and a signature.** Answers will vary.

_____

_____

_____

_____

_____

_____

_____

_____

_____

_____

_____

_____

_____

_____

_____

**MECHANICS**

**UNIT 5** Going West • **Lesson 4** *The Coming of the Long Knives*

# ▶ Structure of a Business Letter

**WRITER'S CRAFT**

Write a letter of complaint to a company that manufactures a product that you have used and had problems with. Remember, a good business letter does the following: 1) tells the reader the letter's purpose, 2) provides reasons why the reader should believe the writer, and 3) lets the reader know what you expect the resolution to be. Find the manufacturer's address on a product package. Include a heading, inside address, salutation, body, closing, and signature in your letter.

Answers will vary. Students should include all six parts of

the business letter.

_____

_____

_____

_____

_____

_____

_____

_____

_____

_____

_____

_____

_____

_____

Name _____ Date _____

# ▶Making Inferences

In the space provided below, write a paragraph or two about a person, a thing, or an event without mentioning the name of your subject. Your goal for this paragraph is to provide clues that will lead your readers to make an important inference about the subject of your paragraph. For example, you might want a reader to infer that the person you write about is a firefighter. You would include clues that the reader could connect to his or her prior knowledge in order to make that inference.

Once you have written your paragraph, trade papers with a classmate. You can make inferences about his or her paragraph, too. Then discuss the paragraphs with one another.

_____

_____

_____

_____

_____

_____

_____

_____

_____

_____

Inference: _____

_____

_____

**COMPREHENSION**

# Words with -ed and -ing

**SPELLING**

## Conventions Strategy

Add *-ed* and *-ing* to the root words below. For each group of words, write a rule for adding *-ed* or *-ing*.

| *Root* | *-ed* | *-ing* |
|---|---|---|
| **1.** play | played | playing |
| **2.** fray | frayed | fraying |
| **3.** Rule | | |

If a word ends in *vowel-y*: add *-ed* or *-ing*

| | | |
|---|---|---|
| **4.** try | tried | trying |
| **5.** cry | cried | crying |
| **6.** Rule | | |

If a word ends in *consonant-y*: change the *y* to an *i* to add *-ed*, do not change the *y* to add *-ing*

| | | |
|---|---|---|
| **7.** ramble | rambled | rambling |
| **8.** balance | balanced | balancing |
| **9.** Rule | If a word ends in a silent *e*: drop the *e* before adding *-ed* or *-ing* | |

| | | |
|---|---|---|
| **10.** tap | tapped | clapping |
| **11.** Rule | If a single-syllable word ends in a short vowel followed by a consonant: double the consonant before adding *-ed* or *-ing*. | |

Name _____ Date _____

 # Similes

**The following sentences contain similes that are overused. Rewrite the sentences with a new simile. Be creative and come up with original similes.**

1. Jamal thought the math test was <u>as easy as pie.</u>

   Answers will vary.

   _____

2. I didn't think Rosa was ever going to make it to the bus stop on time. She's <u>as slow as a turtle.</u>

   Answers will vary.

   _____

3. Winston got an A on the vocabulary test and he's <u>as happy as a clam.</u>

   Answers will vary.

   _____

4. I almost forgot that Cassandra was in the room. She's <u>as quiet as a mouse.</u>

   Answers will vary.

   _____

5. Tara has been working very hard all day long. She's been <u>as busy as a beaver.</u>

   Answers will vary.

   _____

**VOCABULARY**

# ▶ Commas with Independent and Subordinate Clauses

**MECHANICS**

1. Write a sentence with two independent clauses and a coordinating conjunction. **Answers will vary.**

   _____

2. Write a sentence with an independent clause first and a subordinate clause last.

   _____

3. Write a sentence with a subordinate clause first and an independent clause last.

   _____

4. Write a sentence using *but* as a coordinating conjunction.

   _____

5. Write a sentence using *if* as a subordinating conjunction.

   _____

# Tone of a Personal Letter

▶ Describe the tone that you would use for each of the
following friendly letters. **Answers will vary.**

1. A letter thanking your aunt and uncle for money they sent you on
   your birthday. _____

2. A letter to your friend at camp telling him/her what is going on at

   home. _____

3. A letter to your grandparents telling them how you are doing in

   sports/school this year. _____

▶ **Write the body of a letter to a friend telling him/her
about one of the following: vacation/trip, great fear,
favorite book, a time when you got in trouble, awards
or prizes you have won, or new friends you made. At
the end, comment as to the purpose of your letter and
the tone that you used. Explain how one affected the
other.**

_____

_____

_____

_____

_____

_____

_____

**WRITER'S CRAFT**

**UNIT 5**  Going West • **Lesson 6** *Bill Pickett: Rodeo Ridin' Cowboy*

# ▶ Fact and Opinion

**COMPREHENSION**

What is a cowboy? Write your definition of what a cowboy is and then write three other defining statements about a cowboy. Do some research using an encyclopedia, an informational article, or the Internet to find facts about cowboys. Use the information to evaluate whether the statements that you wrote were facts or opinions. Put a check mark in the correct box. Then, adjust your opinion statements to make them factual.   **Answers will vary.**

A cowboy is _____

| Fact | Opinion | Statements and Adjustments |
|------|---------|----------------------------|
| ☐ | ☐ | **1.** Statement: _____<br><br>_____<br><br>Adjustment: _____<br><br>_____ |
| ☐ | ☐ | **2.** Statement: _____<br><br>_____<br><br>Adjustment: _____<br><br>_____ |
| ☐ | ☐ | **3.** Statement: _____<br><br>_____<br><br>Adjustment: _____<br><br>_____ |

*Fact and Opinion* • **Challenge**

Name _____ Date _____

# Words with -er and -est

**Conventions Strategy**

Complete each sentence with one of the words in the box. You will need to add *-er* or *-est* to the words. Use each word once.

| simple | travel | bright | noisy | calm |
|--------|--------|--------|-------|------|
| far | musty | windy | funny | employ |

1. Although it may not be the ___windiest___ city in the United States, Chicago is known as the Windy City.

2. The ___traveler___ boarded the plane with his suitcase in hand.

3. A good ___employer___ treats his or her employees with respect.

4. Terrell started working on the ___simplest___ problems of the math assignment first.

5. The attic, which hadn't been cleaned for years, was probably the ___mustiest___ place I've ever been.

6. LaWanda is always telling jokes; she's one of the ___funniest___ people I know.

7. The North Star is often the ___brightest___ star in the sky.

8. The crowd was at its ___noisiest___ after the team scored the final touchdown.

9. Tonja and I had a contest to see who could throw a ball the ___farthest___.

10. The ocean seemed to be at its ___calmest___ in the morning.

SPELLING

# ►Compound Words

**VOCABULARY**

► Combine a word from row A with a word from row B to form five compound words. Write the combinations and the new words on the lines below.

**Row A:**   book     proof     base     spring     sun

**Row B:**   rise     ball     note     water     time

1. note          + book        = notebook
2. water         + proof       = waterproof
3. base          + ball        = baseball
4. spring        + time        = springtime
5. sun           + rise        = sunrise

► Form four compound words by combining the words in the following box. Then use each new compound word in a sentence.

| spread | case | table | sheet |
|--------|------|-------|-------|
| book   | some | cloth | where |

6. _____

_____

                              Answers will vary.

7. _____

_____

8. _____

_____

9. _____

**UNIT 5** Going West • **Lesson 6** *Bill Pickett: Rodeo Ridin' Cowboy*

# ▶ Commas with Quotation Marks Appositives, Interrupters, and Introductory Words

1. Write a quotation where the question mark comes outside of the quotes.
   **Answers will vary.**
   _____

   _____

2. Write a quotation where the exclamation point comes outside of the quotes.

   _____

   _____

3. Write a dialogue between two of your favorite book characters. Change speakers at least five times. Include an appositive, an introductory word, an interrupter, a question, and an exclamation. Use necessary commas, quotation marks, and end punctuation.

   _____

   _____

   _____

   _____

   _____

   _____

   _____

   _____

   _____

   _____

**UNIT 5**  Going West • **Lesson 7** *McBroom the Rainmaker*

# ▶Cause and Effect

Some effects are also causes that bring about new effects. For example, touching a hot stove (cause) can give you a burn on your hand (effect). In turn, the burn on your hand (cause) could prompt you to run it under cold water (effect). This is called a *cause and effect chain*.

In the spaces below, write other examples of cause and effect chains.

EXAMPLE

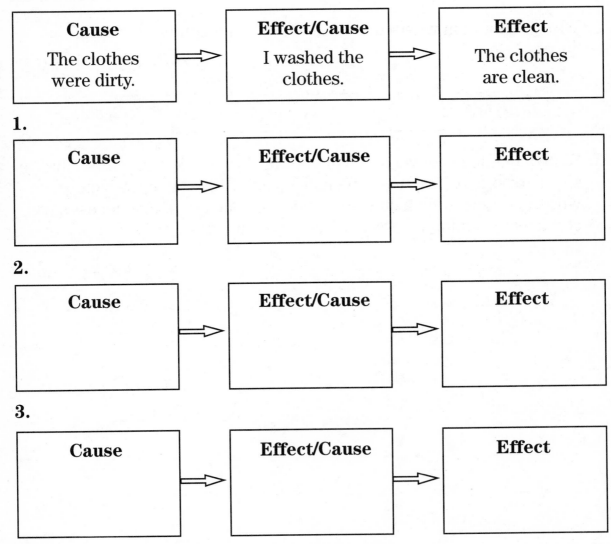

| **Cause**<br>The clothes were dirty. | → | **Effect/Cause**<br>I washed the clothes. | → | **Effect**<br>The clothes are clean. |

1.

| **Cause** | → | **Effect/Cause** | → | **Effect** |

2.

| **Cause** | → | **Effect/Cause** | → | **Effect** |

3.

| **Cause** | → | **Effect/Cause** | → | **Effect** |

*Cause and Effect* • Challenge

# ►Review

## Meaning Strategy

Write two homophones for each word listed.

1. pair __pare__          pear
2. or __oar__          ore
3. poor __pore__          pour
4. sees __seize__          seas
5. to __too__          two

## Conventions Strategy

Add prefixes and/or suffixes to the root word to fit the part of speech and meaning given.

| dis- | mis- | -ent | -ant | -tion | -sion | -sure | -er | -ing | -ed | -est |
|------|------|------|------|-------|-------|-------|-----|------|-----|------|

### ▼Appear

6. verb, to have come into sight __appeared__
7. verb, to come into sight again __reappear__
8. verb, to be in the process of vanishing from sight __disappearing__

### ▼Converse

9. noun, the act of talking together __conversation__
10. noun, familiar or acquainted with __conversant__
11. verb, to be talking together __conversing__

SPELLING

Name _____ Date _____

**VOCABULARY**

# ▶Review

▶For each word, choose the language in the box from which the word originated. Then write a definition. Use a dictionary if necessary.

| Spanish | Italian | French | German |
|---|---|---|---|

1. macaroni: **Italian**
   a food made from a wheat-flour paste or dough

2. polka: **German**
   a lively dance whose basic movement consists of
   three steps and a hop

3. fiesta: **Spanish**
   a festive celebration; holiday

4. fiasco: **Italian**
   a complete failure; disaster

5. cadet: **French**
   a student in a military academy

▶Write two different definitions for each word.

6. mean: a mathematical average

7. mean: to intend to do something

8. difference: the state or quality of being unlike

9. difference: the remainder left after subtracting one quantity

# ▶Review

1. Write a friendly letter to another person in the classroom asking them about their plans for the summer. Be sure to include all the necessary parts of the letter. You will need an additional sheet of paper.

2. Write a business letter to your principal asking him if the class can visit the local historical museum. Be sure to include all the necessary parts of the business letter. You will need an additional sheet of paper.

3. Write three fragments and have a partner turn them into sentences.
   **Answers will vary.**
   _____

   _____

4. Write a sentence with an appositive and have your partner insert the commas.
   _____

5. Write a sentence with an introductory phrase and have your partner insert the commas.
   _____

6. Write a sentence with an introductory clause and have your partner insert the commas.
   _____

7. Write a dialogue changing speakers at least three times.
   _____

   _____

   _____

**GRAMMAR, USAGE, AND MECHANICS**

# ▶ Structure of a Memo

Write a memo using the standard format and the following scenario: You are a member of a scout troop. You are writing to other troops in your area to inform them of the success of a recent fundraiser your troop put together. Include details about the fundraiser, such as how much money was raised and where the money was donated.

Students must use the standard format for writing a memo.

They must also develop the body by beginning with the

most important information and moving on from there. They

should end by stating exactly what action they want taken

and when they want it to occur.

_____

_____

_____

_____

_____

_____

_____

_____

_____

_____

_____

# Sequence

Sequence plays an important role in giving directions. Think about a place you visit frequently. Then write directions for how to get there. You might give directions from school or from your house. Consult a map if necessary. Be sure to use order words so that the sequence of steps in your directions is clear.

**Answers will vary.**

_____

_____

_____

_____

_____

_____

_____

_____

_____

_____

_____

_____

_____

_____

_____

_____

**COMPREHENSION**

# ▶Greek Roots

**Visualization Strategy** Unscramble the letters to write a word to fit the definition given. Use the Greek roots in the box as a guide.

SPELLING

| | | |
|---|---|---|
| **ped** = child | **phys** = nature | **auto** = self |
| **phil** = love | **photo** = light | **meter** = measure |
| **val** = strong | **hydr** = water | **phon** = sounds |

1. eriiancdiatp   **pediatrician**   a doctor who specializes in the needs of children

2. hhooppsiler   **philosopher**   a lover of wisdom

3. orlva   **valor**   outstanding or strong courage

4. ictopgnhoe   **photogenic**   suitable for photographing

5. yhhopondre   **hydrophone**   instrument designed to receive sound waves through water

6. auymtono   **autonomy**   the quality of being self-governing

7. irkloemet   **kilometer**   1,000 meters

8. yuepsiqh   **physique**   the structure or appearance of the body

9. lianavt   **valiant**   characterized by strength, bravery, or courage

10. oghryydlo   **hydrology**   science that deals with water

# ▶Personification

▶The underlined words in the following sentences are examples of personification. Write what is being personified on the first line. Then write two synonyms for the underlined word.

**Answers will vary.**

1. The wind <u>screamed</u> with anger as the lightning flashed.

   **wind**
   _____

   synonyms: **howled** _____ **cried** _____

2. The rabbits <u>waltzed</u> in the garden when the farmer turned his back.

   **rabbits**
   _____

   synonyms: **danced** _____ **pranced** _____

▶Write a sentence using personification with the words given.

3. stars smirk

   **Answers**
   **will vary.**

   _____

   _____

4. elephants rejoice

   _____

   _____

5. volcanoes bristle

   _____

   _____

**VOCABULARY**

Name _____ Date _____

# ▶Review

**GRAMMAR, USAGE, AND MECHANICS**

▶Write the plural form of each noun.

1. governor – elect ___governors – elect___

2. swish ___swishes___

▶Put pronouns in the blanks.    **Answers will vary.**

3. _____ is _____ who will lead _____ nation.

4. _____ grandmother and _____ sister came to visit.

▶Write the correct verb form in the blank using the base verbs in parentheses.

5. Maria ___wished___ (wish) that she could play the clarinet.

6. Breakfast was ___eaten___ (eat) in record time.

▶Write the following types of sentences using proper end marks.
   **Answers will vary.**

7. declarative _____

8. interrogative _____

9. imperative _____

▶Underline the simple subjects and put parentheses around the simple predicate.

10. The <u>children</u>(ran)into the school yard.

11. Around the gym (skipped)the excited <u>cheerleaders</u>.

# ▶ Variety in Writing

**Revise the following paragraph, creating some short emphatic sentences and combining other sentences to create more effective long sentences. Add words or change punctuation, as needed.**

He was bent over at the waist. His gnarly hand rested on a wooden cane. His hand shook ever so slightly. His shoulders were stooped. His thinning, gray hair fell into his eyes as though every strand joined in the effort to propel him down the hallway. He rounded the corner and navigated into the recreation room. At that time a smile appeared on his face because he saw his three friends who loved to play cards. They were already seated. They were waiting for their weekly game of bridge.

Possible rewrites might include:

*He was bent over at the waist, his gnarly hand resting on*

*a wooden cane that shook ever so slightly. His shoulders*

*were stooped, and his thinning gray hair was falling into*

*his eyes as though every strand joined in the effort to*

*propel him down the hallway. As he rounded the corner*

*and navigated into the recreation room, a smile appeared*

*on his face because he saw that his three friends who*

*loved to play cards were already seated and waiting for*

*their weekly game of bridge.*

**WRITER'S CRAFT**

**UNIT 6** Journeys and Quests • **Lesson 2** *Trapped by the Ice!*

# ▶ Latin Roots

**Visualization Strategy** Unscramble the letters to write a word to fit the definition given. Use the Latin roots in the box as a guide.

| | | | |
|---|---|---|---|
| *trans* = across | *anim* = life | *duc* = lead | *cogn* = know |
| *cred* = believe | *pop* = people | *aud* = hear | *firm* = solid |
| *vac* = empty | *hosp* = host | *terr* = land | *laud* = praise |
| *mit* = to send | *port* = carry | | |

1. posrantrt     **transport**     to carry across from one place to another

2. tnsimtra     **transmit**     to send across a distance

3. aanitem     **animate**     to come to life

4. ecnrizeog     **recognize**     to know something from its appearance

5. apiotopuln     **population**     the total number of people in an area

6. direblce     **credible**     capable of being believed

7. rtmafirera     **terra firma**     solid land

8. mucuva     **vacuum**     space devoid of matter

9. ceudtd     **deduct**     to take away or subtract

10. dieuaenc     **audience**     a group of spectators

11. lyatoruda     **laudatory**     containing or expressing praise

12. mtiaanion     **animation**     the quality of being full of life

13. moit     **omit**     to leave out

14. euvaacte     **evacuate**     to leave or vacate

15. bdeulai     **audible**     capable of being heard

**SPELLING**

# ▶ Homophones

Write a homophone for the underlined word in each sentence. Then write a sentence using both homophones. The first one is done for you.

The nurse looked over the list of <u>patients</u>.

1. *patience*

   *It takes a lot of patience to see patients every day.*

My Aunt Betty always tells me how much I've <u>grown</u> since the last time she's seen me.

2. groan

   Answers will vary.

The Giants <u>won</u> the softball game today.

3. one

   Answers will vary.

The <u>herd</u> of elephants was running wild through the jungle.

4. heard

   Answers will vary.

I'm going to ride a <u>horse</u> this afternoon.

5. hoarse

   Answers will vary.

Wipe your <u>feet</u> on the mat before you come inside.

6. feat

   Answers will vary.

**VOCABULARY**

Name _____ Date _____

# ▶Review

**GRAMMAR, USAGE, AND MECHANICS**

▶Write a sentence using a month, a city, a state, and a person's name. Answers will vary.

1. _____

▶Add commas to this heading and inside address.

894 Georgia Way
Atlanta,Georgia 14309
October 14,2001

Ms. Angela Parent
President of Resources
Atlanta Metal Works
789 Forest Boulevard
Atlanta,Georgia 14309

▶Write sentences using the following instructions.

1. Use parentheses. _____

2. Use a hyphen. _____

3. Use a dash. _____

4. Use ellipses. _____

Name _____ Date _____

# ▶ Narrative Paragraphs

A *narrative* paragraph gives the details of an experience or event in story form. The details are included in natural time, or chronological, order. You use narrative form when you tell someone about your day or recall an experience you had. The purpose is to tell a factual or fictional story and describe the action and reactions of the person or participants.

**1.** Fill in the blanks below to write a narrative paragraph.

The first time I ever (skied, babysat, rode a bike, ice skated, etc.) was a total disaster.

**Answers will vary.**

First, _____.

_____

_____

Next, _____

_____

_____

Then, _____

_____

_____

Finally, _____

_____

_____

I had never been more (embarrassed, proud, angry, thrilled, etc.) in my life!

**WRITER'S CRAFT**

# ▶ Words of Spanish Origin

**SPELLING**

**Proofreading Strategy** Read the following paragraphs. Cross out any words that are misspelled and write the correct spelling above the word.

Last summer I went to visit my cousin José in

**ranch**
Mexico. José lives on a ~~rantch~~ with many horses and

**burros**
~~buros~~. Most of the animals spend their days in the

**corral**                          **lassoing**
~~coral~~. José was excellent at ~~lasoing~~ the livestock; I still

need a lot of practice. When we would take walks

**armadillos**
outside, we would often see ~~armadilos~~ burrowing

themselves into the ground.

During the day we usually went to the city and

**plaza**
walked through the ~~plazza~~ . Sometimes we'd eat lunch

**burrito**          **tamale**
in the city. We would get a ~~burito~~, nachos, ~~tamele~~, or

**oregano**
taco. I liked my food spicy with a lot of ~~oregeno~~, salsa,

**jalapeño**
or extra ~~jalapaño~~ peppers.

In the evening we would drive out to the desert

**vista**
where the ~~vissta~~ was beautiful. We would walk

**canyons**                          **mesas**
through the ~~cannyons~~ and climb up to the ~~messas~~. It

was a lot of fun. I hope to go back next summer.

# ▶ Derivations

Write definitions for the following words. Then try to determine the meaning of the Latin root from which the words are derived.

1. secede: to withdraw formally; go away

2. recede: to move back or away

3. precede: to go or come before

4. What do you think the Latin root *ced* means? to go; yield

5. fraction: one or more of equal parts of a whole

6. infraction: breaking or violating something

7. fracture: to cause to come apart

8. What do you think the Latin root *fract* means? to break

9. regime: a prevailing system of administration or rule

10. regulate: to manage or control according to rule

11. regal: befitting a king

12. What do you think the Latin root *reg* means? to rule

13. strict: demanding or observing rigid conformity to rule

14. constrict: to make narrower or smaller

15. restrict: to keep within limits

16. What do you think the Latin root *strict* means? to draw tight, bind

**VOCABULARY**

# ▶Review

## ▶Adjectives and Adverbs

**Underline the adjectives and put the adverbs in parentheses.**

1. Bridget told <u>all</u> guests to gather (quickly) on <u>the</u> <u>back</u> porch.

2. Everyone waited (very) (patiently) for <u>the</u> <u>circus</u> clown.

3. <u>A</u> big <u>black</u> dog raced (excitedly) around <u>the</u> <u>red</u> barn.

## ▶Prepositions

**Write a four sentence paragraph using at least four prepositional phrases.**

Answers will vary.

_____

_____

_____

_____

## ▶Conjunctions and Interjections

**Write a poem at least five lines long. Include three different coordinating conjunctions and one interjection.**

Answers will vary.

_____

_____

_____

_____

_____

_____

# ▶Dialogue

Dialogue is what makes a story come alive. It is conversation in writing. Having characters talk to one another makes a story more believable.

1. Read the selection below, determine the errors, and suggest corrections on the lines below.

   Rachelle and Carolyn decided to go shopping for decorations for their big party. What do you think we should buy? I don't know. Well what about this? Gee, I don't know if they would go with all the other decorations. Well they are the right color. Okay. Let's get them. The two girls went to the cash register.

   It needs quotation marks around words that a person

   speaks. Start a new line each time a different character

   begins speaking. Introduce or follow dialogue with words

   such as *said, replied, commented,* and *remarked,* along

   with the speaker's name. Include details that further

   explain why characters are saying what they say.

2. Continue the story about Rachelle and Carolyn's shopping trip. Write at least two paragraphs that include dialogue with proper punctuation.

   Answers will vary. However, students should start a new

   line each time a different character speaks, introduce

   dialogue with such words as *said, replied,* etc. along with

   the speaker's name, and use correct punctuation.

WRITER'S CRAFT

Name _____ Date _____

# ▶ Author's Purpose

**COMPREHENSION**

On the lines provided below, write two paragraphs. Both
paragraphs will be about the same topic, but each will
have a different purpose. You may choose from the
following purposes for your paragraphs: to inform, to
explain, to entertain, or to persuade. When you are
finished, trade papers with a partner and guess the
purpose of his or her paragraphs.

_____

_____

_____

_____

_____

_____

_____

_____

_____

_____

_____

_____

_____

_____

_____

Name _____ Date _____

# ▶ Words of French Origin

**Pronunciation Strategy** Write the spelling of the word based on the pronunciation. Then write a definition of the word and use it in a sentence. Use a dictionary if necessary.

1. /klar ə net′/ ___clarinet___

   a musical instrument of the woodwind family

   Answers will vary.

2. /kēsh/ ___quiche___

   a rich pie baked with a mixture of cheese, eggs, and cream

   Answers will vary.

3. /bā ə net′/ ___bayonet___

   a large knife or dagger that can be attached to the end of

   a rifle    Answers will vary.

4. /sōō və nîr′/ ___souvenir___

   something kept as a reminder of a person, place, or event

   Answers will vary.

5. /kwi zēn′/ ___cuisine___

   a manner or style of preparing food

   Answers will vary.

6. /krōō′ ton/ ___crouton___

   a small cube of toasted or fried bread

   Answers will vary.

**SPELLING**

**UNIT 6** Journeys and Quests • **Lesson 4** *When Shlemiel Went to Warsaw*

# ▶ Multicultural Words

**VOCABULARY**

Write the definitions for these Yiddish words. Then use them in a sentence.

1. schlep: to carry; especially clumsily or with difficulty _____
   Answers will vary. _____

   _____

2. yarmulke: a skullcap worn by Jewish men and boys _____
   Answers will vary. _____

   _____

3. klutz: an awkward or clumsy person _____
   Answers will vary. _____

   _____

4. chutzpah: shameless impudence; boldness, brazenness _____
   Answers will vary. _____

   _____

5. lox: a smoked, heavily cured salmon _____
   Answers will vary. _____

   _____

# ▶Review

## ▶Independent and Dependent Clauses

Write a four sentence paragraph about the last movie you saw.
Include at least two dependent clauses.   Answers will vary.

_____

_____

_____

_____

## ▶Subject/Verb Agreement, Misused Words, and Double Negatives

Correct this paragraph for subject/verb agreement, misused words, and double negatives.

A cold front is ~~setting too~~ the west. By Sunday
<small>sitting to</small>

night, we may ~~has~~ at least six inches of snow. It will ~~lay~~
<small>have</small>                                              <small>lie</small>

on the ground all week. There won't be ~~no~~ more snow
<small>any</small>

after Sunday.

## ▶Comparative and Superlative Adjectives

1. Write a sentence using the comparative and superlative forms of soft.
   Answers will vary.

_____

## ▶   Direct Objects and Indirect Objects

2. Write a sentence using a compound direct object.
   Answers will vary.

_____

3. Write a sentence using a compound indirect object.

_____

GRAMMAR, USAGE, AND MECHANICS

**WRITER'S CRAFT**

# ▶Effective Beginnings and Endings

**1.** Write an exciting and effective beginning for each topic.

A description of a spooky house   **Answers will vary.**

_____

_____

A friend in trouble

_____

_____

A memory from long ago

_____

_____

**2.** Write an effective ending for each piece of writing described.

An essay about an escaped wild animal

_____

_____

A news report about an accident or fire

_____

_____

A report of a mysterious disappearance

_____

_____

Name _____ Date _____

 # Other Foreign Words

**Foreign Language Strategy** For each word listed, write a definition and write the language from which the word originated. Then use the word in a sentence.

1. cosmonaut: an astronaut, especially a Russian astronaut

   Russian

   Answers will vary.

2. kibbutz: a collective farm or settlement in Israel

   Hebrew

   Answers will vary.

3. gung ho: very enthusiastic; eager

   Chinese/ Mandarin

   Answers will vary.

4. safari: a hunting expedition; especially in Africa

   Arabic/ Swahili

   Answers will vary.

5. aardvark: a burrow-dwelling mammal of south- and

   east-central Africa that has a long, sticky tongue

   Afrikaans/Dutch

   Answers will vary.

SPELLING

# ▶ Metaphor

**VOCABULARY**

▶ **Each sentence contains a metaphor. Explain what the metaphor means.**

1. The little boat was a ping-pong ball being bounced, tossed, and thrown about on the treacherous waves.

   **The boat was being knocked back and forth.**

   _____

2. Alex was a veritable walking encyclopedia when he was asked a question about sports.

   **Alex knows a lot about sports.**

   _____

3. The Giants lost the game and there was nothing they could do about it. It was water under the bridge.

   **It's past and can't be changed.**

   _____

▶ **Write your own metaphors using the words given.**

**Answers will vary. Sample answers given.**

4. clouds cotton

   **The clouds were white, soft cotton balls.**

   _____

5. leaves blanket

   **I lay down on a blanket of leaves.**

   _____

# ▶Review

### ▶Sentences and Fragments

**Write correct after each group of words that is a sentence. If the group of words is a fragment, rewrite it to form a complete sentence.**

1. Sat on the bench in the park. _____ Answers will vary. _____

2. The children ran happily out of school. _ correct _____

3. After crossing the river and climbing the hill. _ Answers will vary. _

### ▶Introductory Clauses

**Write a sentence using this subordinating conjunction.**

4. although _____ Answers will vary. _____

_____

_____

### ▶Capitalization and Punctuation in a Business Letter

**Write a business letter to order a birthday gift for your aunt. Use a separate sheet of paper.** Answers will vary.

### ▶Commas with Coordinating Conjunctions, Appositives, and Introductory Words

Answers will vary.

5. Write a sentence with a coordinating conjunction.

_____

6. Write a sentence with an appositive.

_____

7. Write a sentence with an introductory word.

_____

**GRAMMAR, USAGE, AND MECHANICS**

▶**Suspense**

**WRITER'S CRAFT**

1. On the lines below, write the titles of three stories and three movies (or television shows) you think were suspenseful or surprising. After each title, explain what you thought was suspenseful or surprising about the story, movie, or television show. Finally, write what elements they all seem to have in common.

**Answers will vary. Answers may include that they have**

**sounds that make them suspenseful, they have strong**

**action verbs and vivid description, and/or they suggest**

**danger or mystery.**

_____

_____

_____

_____

_____

_____

_____

_____

_____

_____

# ▶Review

**Foreign Language Strategy** For each word, choose the language in the box from which the word originated. Then write a definition. Use a dictionary if necessary.

| Spanish | Italian | French | German | Chinese | Russian |
|---------|---------|--------|--------|---------|---------|

1. czar: __Russian__
   emperor of Russia; any person with great power

2. boulevard: __French__
   a large city street

3. hamburger: __German__
   a ground beef sandwich

4. spaghetti: __Italian__
   a food consisting of a mixture of wheat flour and dough

5. coyote: __Spanish__
   a wolflike mammal known for its howling at night

6. chopsticks: __Chinese__
   Chinese eating utensils

7. cosmonaut: __Russian__
   an astronaut, especially a Russian astronaut

8. chow mein: __Chinese__
   dish of Chinese-American origin made of
   shredded fish or meat and vegetables

SPELLING

Name _____ Date _____

# ▶Review

▶ **Identify whether the sentence is using personification or a metaphor.**

1. The music danced in my ears as I left the concert hall.
   personification

2. The machine coughed, sighed, and wheezed to a stop.
   personification

3. The stars were shining diamonds that lit up the dark sky.
   metaphor

▶ **Write the Latin root of the following words and its meaning.**

4. secede, recede, precede
   ced                           to go; yield

5. fraction, infraction, fracture
   fract                         to break

6. strict, constrict, restrict
   strict                        to draw tight, bind

▶ **Write the definitions for these Yiddish words.**

7. schlep:    to carry, especially clumsily or with difficulty

8. yarmulke:  a skullcap worn by Jewish men and boys

9. klutz:     an awkward or clumsy person

10. chutzpah: shameless impudence; boldness, brazenness

**VOCABULARY**

*Review* • Challenge

# ▶Review

## ▶Sentences and Punctuation

Write a five sentence paragraph. Include two sentence fragments and three end mark mistakes.

Answers will vary.

_____

_____

_____

_____

## ▶Subjects and Predicates

Underline the simple subject and put parentheses around the simple predicate.

1. <u>Hurricanes</u> in some parts of the world (are called) typhoons or tropical cyclones.

## ▶ Direct Objects and Indirect Objects

▶Rewrite the sentence so it has an indirect object.

2. Harold gave the apple to his mother.
   Harold gave his mother the apple.

## ▶Subject/Verb Agreement

Underline the correct answer.

3. The Marines and the Navy both (uses, <u>use</u>) ships.

4. The days of our summer vacation (goes, <u>go</u>) by too fast.

5. Which one of the stores (<u>has</u>, have) the type of shirt you like?

GRAMMAR, USAGE, AND MECHANICS

**WRITER'S CRAFT**

# ▶ Point of View

One story can be told in two ways. It can be told by using a first-person narrator. This means an *I* is telling a story about something that happened to him or her. A story can also be told from someone else's point of view, which is third-person narration. The voice would use third-person pronouns like *she* or *he*.

Think of a story you have recently read. Notice which narrative voice the author used. Tell why the author might have chosen that voice. How would the story have been different if the voice had been changed? Write your comments on the lines below.

**Answers may vary.**

_____

_____

_____

_____

_____

_____

_____

_____

_____

_____

_____

_____

*Point of View* • Challenge